"David, listen carefully."

When you say *home*, I'll take you home. It's very easy. You can laugh, so open your mouth, take a deep breath, and say *home*. Go ahead. David, no one can do it for you. You have to say the first word, then others will follow. Right now—say *home*. He opened his mouth and faintly whispered *home*.

"David's story is moving, but he shares the limelight with a mother who kept demanding more from him and from those who worked with him. . . . Her achievements—and his—are undeniable."   *—Kirkus Reviews*

DAVID

A Mother's Story of Her Son's Recovery from a Coma and Brain Damage

by Dorothy Landvater

A KANGAROO BOOK
PUBLISHED BY POCKET BOOKS NEW YORK

DAVID

Prentice-Hall edition published 1976

POCKET BOOK edition published November, 1977

This POCKET BOOK edition includes every word contained in
the original, higher-priced edition. It is printed from brand-
new plates made from completely reset, clear, easy-to-read type.
POCKET BOOK editions are published by
POCKET BOOKS,
a Simon & Schuster Division of
GULF & WESTERN CORPORATION
1230 Avenue of the Americas,
New York, N.Y. 10020.
Trademarks registered in the United States
and other countries.

Dedication

This book is for those
    who face a crisis.
May they have the strength
    to take a step at a time.
For with each step comes
    hope, courage, faith,
and the realization that
    with God's help,
nothing is insurmountable.

Acknowledgments

I cannot possibly list by name the persons to whom I would like to express my thanks, for as surely as the sun rises and sets I would unintentionally miss one and that would distress me, but you know who you are.

With all my heart I sincerely say: I am everlastingly grateful to *you*.

PART ONE

Overlook Hospital

ICU

It was 9:30 P.M. I was beat! For some reason I consider it my wifely duty to wash, starch, and iron my husband's shirts; one of those mother-to-daughter things. Finished. I gathered them together and slowly climbed the stairs. The phone rang.

"John! Can you get it?"

When I heard him say, "I'll call the hospital and give my permission," I stopped, paralyzed.

"Okay," he said, and hung up.

"That was the police. David had an accident with my car. We're to go to Overlook Hospital right away. They need our permission to treat him."

Weak with fear, I clutched the freshly ironed shirts. My mother instinct saw blood, broken bones, knocked-out teeth, the whole bit. But that small inner voice I've been living with for forty-five years cut in—"Don't panic! Get the facts first."

"Why did the police call us?"

"The hospital didn't have our number."

"Well for heaven's sake, David knows his own number. Unless . . ."

A dreadful silence filled the car as we sped to Summit. It took only fifteen minutes, but seemed like an hour. As the parents of four sons, and living in Berkeley Heights ten years, we're known as regulars in emergency. The doctor on call walked toward us, put his arm around me, and said, "I'm so sorry. I've already taken the liberty of calling in a neurologist."

A youngish, small man with tense, wet facial muscles stepped forward.

"Your son was brought in by ambulance unconscious. We've X-rayed his neck and jaw but found nothing. I need your permission to go on."

"You have it," John answered.

I cut in, "I'd like Dr. Costabile called. He's our family doctor."

"Of course, we'll do it immediately."

"May I see David?"

The doctor put out his hand to stop two nurses who were pushing him around the corner on a stretcher. David was stripped to the waist. No blood, no visible marks of any kind, only a bottle of IV running into his arm. His pants weren't torn. Even his sandals were like new.

Relief flooded over me. "He's just knocked out," I thought.

John and I waited in X-ray.

"David asked for your Volkswagen to date Kim," I muttered. "Where do you suppose she is?"

"He was going to her house. Someone said the car had spun across the road and wrapped around a tree. It was headed toward home."

"And to think we wouldn't let him buy a motor-cycle."

I could see David standing before me only a few hours ago, showered and dressed. Although it was drizzling rain I didn't remind him to be careful. Instead, I remembered asking, "Where did you get that shirt?"

"It's Zack's. Kim likes me in blue."

"Hmmm . . . Well, don't stay late. You have to work tomorrow."

He had a summer job with the same landscaper his brother Darryl had worked for two years ago. When David first started he complained that every muscle ached—even soaked in a tub of Epsom salt—but now he was "in condition," with a beautiful tan and his blond hair almost white.

Jolting me back to reality, our family doctor stood before us.

"This is serious," he said. "He has a brain stem concussion and is in a coma. We don't know how long it will be until he wakes up. They've taken him to the Intensive Care Unit. It's on the ninth floor."

Have you even been in an intensive care unit? I never had. Four beds were in the room. David's was the first inside the door. The lighting was dim and a piercing beep came from a small TV monitoring heart and pulse rate. I watched the swinging needle, not knowing if it was recording something good or bad. The atmosphere reeked efficiency as soft-footed, sterile nurses hovered over David, checking and rechecking his vital signs. An oxygen mask had been added, a catheter, and several more bottles. I felt very much in the way but couldn't bring myself to leave. It was unreal. Eventually we went home.

Sleep was impossible. "God," I asked, "you wouldn't take my seventeen-year-old boy, would you?"

Instantly the word *time* repeated itself like a broken record until sleep took over.

The following morning at 6 A.M. I called for a report. "No change." Two little words and then the connection broke.

I telephoned our son Darryl. I had called after we came home from the hospital, letting it ring and ring, but no one answered. Now he and his wife, Barb, arrived within minutes. Fear, tension, and confusion hung heavy. When the unexpected happens you don't know what to do first. Oh, how I longed to pick up a book and read ten easy instructions on how to cope with a crisis. It was decided that John, Darryl, and Barb would see David before going to work. I forced myself to make a few necessary phone calls.

At 10 A.M. our minister met me in the hospital lobby. Dean was brand-new to our church and had never met David. Together we went to the ninth-floor waiting room. Another neurologist (three were in the same office; this doctor lived on our street) and our family doctor walked in. The specialist spoke.

"Nothing looks good. His temperature rose to 107 degrees Fahrenheit during the night. He's on an ice blanket to keep it down, but remains extremely spastic and has sunk deeper into the coma. All indications point to heavy brain damage. Things don't look good, but of course there is always hope."

"You know," I said, "it was your dog that bit our David."

Funny the things one blurts out during a time of stress. It had happened about seven years ago. The comment broke the icy atmosphere, but only for a moment.

Dean and I saw David. A nurse stood with us. "He looks just asleep," I whispered. Dean nodded.

"He's such a handsome boy," the nurse added.

Surely, I thought, that awful diagnosis must be wrong. I didn't really believe our family doctor agreed with the specialist. There was something about the way he stood there with his hand over his mouth. I had expected him to say something, but he never did. Last night he kept repeating, "He'll come out of this, you'll see."

Looking down at David, I was positive. Today, in fact any minute now, he would wake up and yell, "I'm hungry!" He was always snooping around for food, especially sweets.

Our ten minutes were up. We left and went to chapel.

Both of us, each in our own way, asked for God's help. One thing I knew for certain—we were not alone. I felt His words rush forward filling the small chapel:

Where two or three are gathered in my name, there am I in their midst.

I returned to the lobby where my friends were waiting. There was Lois. Frank had answered my call. "I don't know what Lois has on for today," he said, "but she'll be there."

Charlotte was there too. She knew what I was going through. Only a few years ago her husband had a near-fatal accident on Route 22. "I came to help," she said. "What can I do?"

"I don't know. I can't think."

"I'll bring dinner tonight. You've got to eat."

"Something light, you know my lousy colon."

"Let me handle everything."

At twelve noon our third son, Lance, arrived from college. When I called in the morning to say, "You'd better come home," he left Pennsylvania immediately. Lance, a second-year premed student at Franklin and Marshall, was working on an ecology project for the summer.

We saw David together. A nurse stood with us.

"Why is his right hand fisted up to his chin?" Lance asked.

"That's a result of the accident. It's locked. We've rolled washcloths and forced them into his fists so they won't tighten more."

We didn't fully understand it, but were grateful for each and every thing they did for David. We returned to the lobby. Kim and many of David's school friends were waiting. I was surrounded by people.

At 3 P.M. that small inner voice cried, "Greg must be told." Our second son, age twenty-one, had hit the road in June, traveling across the country. His decision upset us all. I remembered saying, "Keep in touch. I'll worry—where will you sleep, what will you eat, and suppose something happens to you or to someone at home?" I walked to the pay phone and dialed our local police. They teletyped an alert to thirteen states.

*   *   *

After David's accident on July 20, 1972, our life style changed. My hospital vigil started at 10 A.M. The family arrived at 6 P.M., and after they saw David we went home for dinner. We returned for the 8 and 10 P.M. visits, never missing our precious ten minutes every two hours. Darryl, Barb, and Lance went back throughout the night. We all knew we had to be there when David woke up. Each morning at 6 A.M. I called for a report.

"No change." Her voice was sterile.

On the third day the neurologist said the coma had slightly lightened from when David was admitted. We were most encouraged.

Sunday, for the first time, I attended services in the hospital chapel. Preceding the prayer the chaplain confessed, "I haven't met all of you personally, but I know your individual needs and especially pray for you." He looked straight at me. After services we talked. "Don't be afraid to call on God when you need him," he said. "Be honest, too. If you want David as he was before the accident, then ask for that."

A young chaplain who was in training for the summer had also been counseling me. David was his first case. Early every morning he'd come through the lobby looking for me, as well as stopping by "our corner" during the day. It was he who brought us the news that the coma had lightened. Other ministers began to stop by too, some I knew and some I did not. I was touched and secure in the knowledge that so many wanted to help.

Three days had passed and no word from Greg. John appealed to the AP wire service. They accepted an article and a picture which a friend hand-carried to the Newark office. Four local papers printed a headline story—"Son Critically Ill—Parents Looking for Brother." Surely now someone would find Greg.

* * *

Tuesday, David's color was a frightening blue-gray as he labored for every breath. It was awful to watch. Terribly worried, I begged the nurse, "Can't you do something for him?"

"A pulmonary specialist has been called." I relaxed some.

Another complication developed—profuse internal bleeding. The doctors met in consultation. Decision: stop the cortisone. Cortisone was the most effective drug to reduce edema, but now they had to switch.

It was a tense day, and when we pushed the button to enter ICU at 8 P.M. a voice answered, "Visitors for David please wait in the waiting room. The doctors are with him."

It was a small, close room with a heavy atmosphere —a woman was lying on the sofa sobbing her heart out. No one talked. What could we say? Suddenly Barb got up and with a strong, swift movement shoved the black, fake-flower arrangement underneath the table. I guess some decorator thought black plastic flowers in an orange vase added that perfect touch to the decor. For Barb, they had to go.

By 9:30 P.M. our family doctor announced, "We've got the bleeding under control; now I'll do the tracheotomy."

"Where will you do it?" I asked.

"Right on the bed. I can't risk moving him."

Our family doctor is a surgeon. Eventually we all went home, at least content with the fact that we saw David breathing easier and the urine in the bag was no longer bright red.

The following morning a group of people in white surrounded David's bed. They made me nervous. The nurse explained—they were observing. The pulmonary specialist had put his ear to David's chest and detected a possible collapsed lung. He ordered a chest X-ray.

David looked dreadful. His face and neck were puffed out twice their size. Since the tracheotomy it seemed a hundred times a day the nurses slipped on gloves, inserted a tube down his trachea, and sucked out the mucus. At first I thought of running from the room, but stood still with a pained look as his body jerked in protest. When I left the big X-ray machine was being rolled in.

At 8 P.M. the cold words came over the intercom again—"Visitors for David, please wait in the waiting room."

"Why?" we asked each other. "What has happened?"

Time dragged. Someone had rescued the black fake flowers. I hid them in the corner. Two hours later our family doctor explained that the lower lobe of his left lung had collapsed. He performed surgery, inserted a tube into the collapsed lobe, and added a machine to inflate the lung. "Hang in there," he said. "He'll make it."

The next night our fingers never pressed the button to enter ICU—a nurse was waiting for us. With a compassionate, apologetic voice she told us the upper lobe of David's right lung had collapsed. We were to wait in the waiting room while our family doctor repeated the procedure.

Did you ever watch the clock for two hours? Nerve-racking, isn't it? Finally at 10 P.M. we saw David. He looked like a robot—a machine for each lung, plus all the other apparatus. Afraid, but wanting to know, I asked, "Doctor, is it possible the other lobes will collapse too?"

"That is a possibility we face. At this point we are mostly concerned with pneumonia setting in. We're calling in another specialist."

All doctors met in consultation. Decision: bronchoscopy.

For the fourth consecutive night at 8 P.M. we wore out the hours in the waiting room. We named it the crying room because someone was always crying. Meanwhile, our friends sat downstairs in the main lobby sending their prayers and energy to David and to us. Just knowing that made us feel somewhat better.

The new specialist pried David's mouth open and inserted a pipe down his throat to the lungs. He saw the feared fluid and drew it out.

By this time even the black fake flowers no longer bothered us. We left them on the table. Each felt totally drained with the gnawing question—what will tomorrow night bring? And when the nightly phone call came from my father asking, "Well, how's our boy doing?" I hated to answer.

Hope sprang in the morning. Those observing David were smiling. His lower left lobe had inflated. The machine was removed and the wound sutured. Another day passed and the other lung inflated. After ten days David was stabilizing.

That evening as we rode the elevator down with our family doctor, he admitted, "This kid's almost given me a heart attack, but he's gonna make it. I don't see what else can go wrong. It's just a matter of time now. I'm leaving day after tomorrow on vacation."

We knew he had stayed over the weekend for David. As a matter of fact, John and I had planned to spend July 21, 22, and 23 with the doctor and his wife at their summer home, until the accident happened. Today, deep down inside, I was selfishly hating to see him go until September 1.

Three days later a new surgeon was called. They were running out of places to insert the IV needle. A subclavian cut-down was done and the nurses assured me it would hold as long as intravenous feedings were needed.

At home, my house had been cleaned several times over. Dry cleaning was delivered, laundry done, and the refrigerator stocked. Each night I was warmed all over as I read the yellow pad by the telephone. One sheet listed the volunteers scheduled to answer the phone day and night in the event Greg called. David's friends were taking the night shift. The second sheet listed those catering food. Since the accident I hadn't cooked one meal. Phone calls flooded in early morning and late at night, but I never felt like saying, "Oh, leave me alone!" I needed the cards, notes, books, telegrams, flowers, fruit, and the people who circled me like a cocoon. I was never alone at the hospital either. Even the night guards were sympathetic. They left the lights on after 9 P.M. so Barb could knit. Hours melted into days. David was now in his thirteenth day of the coma.

Wherever I was—elevator, coffee shop, lobby—people asked, "Are you the mother of the boy in the coma?"

"Yes."

"How is he doing?"

"About the same."

"I'll say a prayer for him."

"Thank you. I really appreciate it."

The telephone operators and desk receptionists told me daily of the constant stream of calls asking David's condition. Two in particular called every day—Clover Hill Swim Club and the Webers. I had already received a note from the Webers. David's accident occurred on their lawn and they had called the ambulance.

Even the director of Overlook Hospital said, "Not often, but every once in a while the whole hospital becomes caught up with a case. This is certainly true of David."

One morning as I entered ICU a young man in a white uniform was standing by David's bed.

"Are you his mother?"

"Yes."

"I work here as an orderly and ever since he was brought in I come every morning to offer my prayer."

Again and again I was lifted by others.

And then I will never forget Mrs. Miller. Her husband had been in and out of hospitals for years.

"My faith has been the only thing that has kept me going," she said. "What do people do who have none?"

Beginning tomorrow I'm going to offer a prayer to St.
Jude, the patron of hopeless cases, for David."

"That's nice of you. May I have a copy or is that
a no-no? I'm Protestant."

"Of course not. We'll say the novena for nine days."

Time passed. It was no longer July, and still no
word from our son Greg. I sent out a news release
to twenty underground newspapers. I also notified
Lehigh University, where Greg had been a student.
This done, I was confident that somehow, someone
would find Greg.

Red letter day—August 9. The doctors had scheduled a test—a cerebral angiogram. Everything was
synchronized. Two nurses plus an oxygen tank marched
along to X-ray. Dye was shot into David's brain to
determine if there was a blockage. John rushed in
from work to hear the results. There was no blockage
or blood clot, and surgery would not be necessary.
We were thankful.

Our family never felt ill at ease because David was
unconscious. We'd pick up his hand and talk directly
to him, rattling on and on about everyday family
affairs, the weather, the people who were downstairs,
his friends, anything that came to our minds. Every
day after work Barb would go with me for the 4 P.M.
visit, giving her news. We all believed David knew we
were there.

Many times during the midnight visit Lance took
Kim or one of David's friends. Actually, the night
nurses suggested it, hoping one of his peers would
trigger a response. It was a traumatic experience for
these young people, but their desire to help gave them
strength and they returned again and again.

I received a second note from the Webers, saying
they had circulated a petition to their neighbors and
all had signed. The petition stated the road area was
prone to accident, David's being the third serious one,

with countless other close calls. They were asking the county engineer to consider signs designating existing road conditions, lowering the speed limit, a solid line prohibiting passing, and improved shoulders.

The residents won their case and a copy of both letters was enclosed. I vowed and declared someday David and I would ring their doorbell and thank them in person.

August 11, as I entered ICU, the atmosphere around David was changed—more quiet. My eyes flitted around—what was it? Then I saw the repetitious beeper box that recorded heart and pulse rate was gone. I smiled, happy to see progress.

August 20, one month to the day after his accident, as I made my 10 A.M. visit I sensed danger. It was so real I could feel it in the air. With a frightened, shaky voice I called, "Nurse, is David all right?"

"He was a minute ago."

"He doesn't look it now. I don't think he's breathing."

Immediately she was at David's side, checking. "It's just a little shallow."

"Call the doctor," I pleaded.

"Suppose you step outside now." Her voice told me they'd handle everything. As I headed for the crying room the public address system was paging the pulmonary specialist. Within ten minutes I was called back. Currents of fear were shooting through me and my heart was galloping dangerously. But then the word *time* rushed forward in my mind.

Facing the pulmonary specialist, I cried, "What happened?"

"We don't know. For some unknown reason he stopped breathing. He's on a respirator now. If it's temporary we can cope with it. If it's a paralysis, this is the end. It's a giant step backward."

I couldn't believe it. I dragged my crushed body back to the crying room. Immediately, everyone knew. The hospital chaplain took me into his office.

"I'm sure by now you have learned to pray and don't need me."

"Oh, but I do."

I'll never forget his closing words. "And now, oh God, I ask what she dare not. In the event it goes the other way, give her the strength she will need."

As I left his office a friend came rushing down the hall.

"I came as soon as I heard."

I merely nodded. My head was spinning; I felt weak. "Have you got one of those little yellow tranquilizers I refused the first day?"

"Yes, and it's about time you took one."

We returned to the lobby. Mrs. Miller was waiting. "Dottie, I just don't understand it. Today was the last day to give our prayer to St. Jude. Already I told him off. 'Listen,' I said, 'I didn't ask you to make the boy worse. I want him better.'"

My friends and I exchanged glances. We felt the same way she did, but her indignant tone to St. Jude brought a smile to our sad faces. Every two hours for ten minutes when I saw David I picked up his hand, pleading with all my might, "Fight, David, come on, you're strong as a bull. You can't give up now. Breathe, breathe, breathe." Before leaving, my eyes checked the respirator. All buttons were deadly silent. Only the swish of the big bellows as it inhaled and exhaled for David could be heard.

3 P.M.—no change. My fears doubled, tripled. I called the family. We went in together. "Oh, look," I whispered, "a light is flashing."

"It's only recording a sigh, Mom."

Between visits we waited in the crying room. No one spoke. We were completely absorbed in our own thoughts, and afraid to discuss them. At 6 P.M. the assist button flashed once. Now we could talk. Our pent-up emotions overflowed to one another. After eight tense, endless hours David began to respond erratically. We hung onto hope stronger than ever. At 10 P.M. David assisted the respirator in a regular pattern. Weak and exhausted, but thanking God, we went home.

A day and a half later the machine was disconnected, but not removed.

A whole month with only glucose had caused the pounds to melt away. David's vertebrae looked like a skeleton—a hotbed for sores. A tube feeding through the nose had been tried but his digestive system rejected it. We were told the first thing to return would be his body thermostat, which controlled his temperature. With anxious eyes we checked the refrigeration unit at the foot of his bed. Once it was off. Certain it was a turning point for David, we told one and all. But the very next visit, only two hours later, it was back on. At moments like this I was disappointed but held it to a surface disappointment. From the time of the accident I refused to let myself become hysterically upset. Time was of the essence and I knew I couldn't afford to waste it. I was like a sitting duck at a carnival —shot down, I'd always bounce up again.

Helpful friends felt they needed to take the bull by the horns.

"Dottie, you can't keep living at this hospital."

"Why not?"

"Because he might be in a coma for a long time."

"What do you suggest I do?"

"Go out. Anything, but get away from this atmosphere."

They didn't understand. What would I do at home? However, I did agree to go out for lunch with them after I saw David at noon if they returned me in time for the 2 P.M. visit. From then on I was royally wined and dined. There seemed no end to people's generosity.

Bless my friend Luella, she knew how I felt. Every morning when I stepped off the elevator after seeing David, Luella would be sitting on the bench with a smile. On tense days she'd gather others and we'd march into chapel, repeating the novena or our individual prayers. On so-so days we'd have tea and a flattened hard roll in the coffee shop. I needed her strength and I took it.

Red letter day—August 25. My whole body felt charged with excitement and my voice grew high-pitched with enthusiasm as I announced to the neurologist, "David hears me!"

"Oh, I think not. You're letting your imagination run wild. That's understandable."

"No, listen. I told him to blink his eyes once if he heard me and he did."

"I'm sure it was a reflex."

My voice dropped an octave and so did my attitude as I rushed on with stubborn determination. "Doctor, I am in this hospital every day. I live here! You come a couple times a week for a total of two to three minutes. I tell you, he hears me!"

Boy, was I mad. My heart was thumping and my face was beet red as I hurried down the hall to Luella. I knew I was shouting at her, "I know David hears me but that doctor won't believe me! How can he be so sure I'm wrong?" Suddenly Luella began wildly gesturing. I turned and faced the neurologist.

"I have reexamined David. I asked him to blink his eyes twice if he heard me, and he did. You might be right."

The next day David's condition was changed from critical poor to critical fair and the IV needle was removed for good. His body was accepting tube feedings. We were pleased, the nurses were pleased, and our family doctor was pleased. He was back from his vacation. At 10 A.M. I was asked to wait a few minutes because the nurses had a surprise for me. When I entered ICU I didn't know whether to laugh or cry as I knelt to embrace David. He was sitting in a chair. Sitting is a loose term. His limp body was tied at the head, shoulders, and waist. His feet, cuddled in lamb's wool, were propped on a stool, and all exposed parts were wrapped in a sheet blanket. It had taken three nurses ten minutes to get him up. Everyone, our family doctor included, happily gathered around, shouting words of encouragement to David. It was a tremendous step of progress, and from then on the new orders were that he was to be out in a chair twice a day.

Inhalation therapy was also begun. David tried to fight the rubber mask that fit over his face. Although he couldn't move his facial muscles his eyes were expressive. They seemed to say, "I don't like this thing, take it away."

The nurses took great pride in brushing David's blond hair straight out over the pillow. Now that his glands were beginning to function again, it was oily, and they washed it. But the truth was, he needed a haircut. Before his accident long hair was his hang-up. Either Kim or I was allowed to cut it. What a hassle! He'd stand before the mirror with all lights on and with each fraction of an inch yell, "Stop—too much—stop." We were positive when he saw me with scissors in hand he'd wake up. Kim held his wobbly head and I snip-snipped.

"David, your mother's cutting your hair. You'd better let her know how much you want off."

But David was oblivious. It made us feel guilty.

August 26. The mouth prop that protected his teeth from grinding was removed. That evening I marched in with David's toothbrush—not a new one either, but his old yellow one from home. No more dragon breath.

Two days later his body thermostat had repaired itself. No more ice blanket. He had been lying on it for a total of thirty-five days, and in the beginning had had one top and bottom. It was replaced with an electrically controlled air mattress. The coils automatically shifted under his body to relieve pressure and hopefully prevent bedsores.

Since the first of August David's eyes had begun to open, at first just a slit. When they were fully open I called the neurologist. Charged with excitement, my words tumbled on top of each other. "Doctor, David sees me! Honest."

"Not really. He now has an awake and a sleep period in the coma."

Shot down again, I appealed to the nurses. They were reluctant to comment, but I noticed they observed David more closely when I was in the room. Now they too saw his eyes following as they tube-fed him. Immediately I rushed right in with two 8-by-10 pictures David had taken, developed, and mounted. One was a close-up of Herbert, his girl cat, and the other was of Kim.

"David, do you know who this is? If you do, blink your eyes once." I held up Herbert's picture.

His eyes blinked once. I felt warm and deliriously happy. I repeated the same procedure for Kim's picture, then asked, "David, did you take both pictures?"

His eyes blinked once.

"David, I've known all along you could understand us. Remember I told you that you had an accident with your father's car and you're in Overlook Hospital?"

His eyes blinked once.

"You're gonna be okay, just hang in there."

The nurses and I were delighted with this recall. We propped the pictures on the refrigeration unit at the foot of his bed so he could see them all day.

My friend Isabelle had clipped an article from a magazine telling about patients who were brought out of comas by playing continuous music. I discussed it with the family. Darryl's reaction was, "I'll be no part of your scheme, Mom." I had to try it anyway. With my tape recorder tucked under my arm, I walked into ICU oozing self-confidence. Not really—I was shaking in my shoes. I'm not sure what it is, but there is something about specialists that causes me to become unglued. I hate to admit it's fear. Perhaps it's just that I didn't want to believe what they continually told me. The nurses came to my rescue and told the neurologist my plan.

He called for me. "Let's see what happens when you

turn it on." The nurse inserted the plug in David's ear and I flipped the On button.

His whole body began to jerk and move.

"It seems he's responding. I see no reason for you not to use it, unless the nurses feel they don't have time to keep it running."

"We'll do it," they chorused.

The young chaplain's training period was over. I would miss him. I had watched him become more and more involved with David and our family as the weeks passed. And when he handed me a perfect, single yellow rose, I knew his prayers and thoughts would continue even though he was leaving.

Six weeks after the accident the neurologist reported, "David will live but we have reasons to believe he will be a vegetable. All the encephalograms show very abnormal brain patterns, indicating the cells above the brain stem are also damaged. He has lost his entire motor control; his right side is more affected than his left. He now needs therapy, therefore I am asking the doctor of rehabilitation to see him."

It seemed to me every time the neurologist opened his mouth words of gloom came out. If I questioned him he would retort, "Don't ask me a question you've already answered in your own mind." And yet only that morning the pulmonary specialist who never commented said, "I think he's getting better." Practically every morning at 10 A.M. I found him examining David. As I watched him handle David and other patients in the room, I was glad that he had been called in on the case, and today when he spoke, my dampened spirits were lifted. Driving home I asked, "You didn't let him live to be a vegetable, did you, God?"

"Be still and know that I am God," rushed forward. I accepted those words and that was that.

When I arrived home there was a volunteer with our dinner. Six weeks and still I hadn't cooked one meal.

I'm sure you've heard the cliché, "People today don't want to become involved; they really don't care." Not so. It was incredible. One person told another; many I never knew. All joined together for David. Letters had been written to Norman Vincent Peale, Billy Graham, Oral Roberts, and Kathryn Kuhlman. Candles were burning and prayer chains were circling all over. Even the man who laid the tile in our bathroom began one in his church. And those who believed in psychic healing groups were working for David. We were thankful for each and every one.

Barb had been keeping notes on a brown paper bag. On September 4 she recorded, "Davie really recognized our presence today. A special high-backed wheelchair arrived, bought for him. He ate sherbet and applesauce fed with a spoon."

Up to this time David could not talk because of his trach, but the nurses and I were sure on occasion we had heard him make a noise using his vocal cords. Everyone gathered around as the pulmonary specialist corked his trach, each expecting, hoping, praying he would say something.

"David, you can talk now. Say something to me. Anything, like, 'Mom, hi, Dot—go ahead.' "

We waited with bated breath. Nothing. All of us tried again and again, but no sound came from David. Our eyes met. We silently shouted to each other the ugly truth—David could not talk.

"Doctor, do you consider David out of the coma now?"

"That's a hard question to answer. The coma continues to lighten."

"I always thought one day he would just wake up."

"In his case it will be very gradual. He will never have a day of awakening."

I didn't fully understand it, but I accepted it. David had come so far and I believed he would go farther. My attitude of "nothing is insurmountable" took over.

*   *   *

Range-of-motion exercises to all four extremities were started by a physical therapist in ICU. The nurses and I were told to observe while the speech therapist instructed feeding. David was propped up with two people supporting his head.

"In cases this bad," said the therapist, "you force the mouth open by rubbing a spoon across the lips." Her voice was clipped and rapid. "Place the finger food on his left side between cheek and gum. Rotate the cheek on the outside with your finger to promote chewing. Massage his Adam's apple and he will swallow." She fed David a graham cracker dipped in applesauce.

Her theory worked, but I hated her. It was the words "in cases this bad." What a sour viewpoint. Besides, David could hear.

The following morning the nurse was beaming when I entered ICU. "I got a whole soft-cooked egg in him for breakfast. It took half an hour but I did it."

I loved her.

Red letter day—September 11. The trach was permanently removed. Fifty-three days had passed since the accident. They had been traumatic and tense days. In the beginning I felt like my body didn't belong to me—it functioned automatically. I ate because everyone fussed: "You must eat." I wanted someone to shake me and say, "It's all over. You've had a bad dream, wake up." But no one did. David's accident was real. I had lived it. And now after fifty-three days, good news had arrived. David was taken off the critical list.

A word must be said about all those who worked with David in ICU. They were amazing! Not once did they show pessimism, annoyance, or fear to me. The tender, loving care they gave David was real. I know because I was there every two hours for ten minutes. Often they let me stay longer as they saw David responding. Not one bedsore, either—proof of their constant turning and care of his skin. By now we estimated David had lost forty pounds. And from the start they always spoke to him as if they knew he fully understood. Fifty-three days is a long time, and they had become attached to David. When we left everyone was happy but a little sad too. I wished I could do something for them and then I realized what would make them most happy would be to see David walking and talking. Someday we'd come back. In the meantime, I proudly presented a homemade cheese-cake and a batch of fudge from David, via me. He used to make it all the time. It always turned out perfect. Mine was overcooked.

SPECIAL CARE

I have seen many patients moved from ICU. For those to whom God gave final peace I sorrowed. Each one touched me personally. For those who moved down the hall to Special Care I felt joy, saying over and over, "David's day will come!"

It came. September 12—the day after David was taken off the critical list.

I tasted panic! Call it mother's overprotectiveness, but he was "our miracle." Even the tap of my heels seemed to echo "I hope they're doing the right thing" as David's bed moved down the hall and around the corner to Room 915.

Special Care is a unit for patients who are off the critical list but remain seriously ill. They require close observation and specialized nursing care. Visitors are limited to the immediate family. David was placed in a semiprivate room next to the nurses' station.

At this point the neurologist reported, "David remains comatose. The prognosis: He will have to be retaught speech and his vocabulary will be limited; his right side's a serious problem and I don't think he will ever regain the use of his right arm; he'll walk, but dragging his right leg. Of course, our main concern is his mind."

It was not a glowing report, but I had been taking it a day at a time, sometimes an hour at a time. David had life and no one could tell me differently—hope followed.

My daily routine changed. I rushed into the lobby at 8:15 A.M. proudly clutching an insulated ice cream bag and stepped into the elevator.

"Hi, David. I brought your favorite breakfast— Czechoslovakian pancakes. Let's see what the hospital sent you. Cooked cereal—chuck-up food! Isn't that what you always called it?"

His eyes blinked once. Each time I pushed for recall, David came through. I smiled, pleased as punch.

"Need my help?" asked the nurse.

"I'd be grateful if you could hold his head up."

I broke a small piece from the pancake, placed it inside his left cheek, and rotated the area on the outside, all the while praying, "Please God, don't let him choke on my pancakes." Half an hour later all three were eaten. As only a mother can tell, he liked them.

The occupational therapist came during teeth-brushing time. She carried a shallow box with four round, plastic, colored balls.

"David, do you see a red ball inside this box?"

His eyes blinked once.

"Point to it. Reach out your left hand and touch the red ball."

Time rushed by. No one spoke. We waited and waited what seemed a silent eternity and then his whole body tensed and jerked as the left hand moved ever so slightly. I was spellbound. Have you ever thought about the amount of effort it takes to move your arm? I never had. Over and over I kept saying to myself, "Come on, you can do it. You're strong as a bull."

"That's right," she said. "Now point to the yellow ball."

It took half an hour but he pointed to all four colors. I was ecstatic! He not only remembered colors, he saw them and could follow instructions.

Three nurses entered. "David, we're going to take you downstairs to therapy now."

One held his head, one supported his back, and the other picked up his feet as they slid him onto a stretcher and marched off. I tagged along. The physical therapist helped transfer him onto the tilt table. She anchored his feet in metal braces lined with lamb's wool and tilted him forward. Instantly, without speech or any facial expression, we all sensed from the look in his eyes that he wanted off. His left hand tried to move to the straps that held him on.

Turning to me, the therapist explained, "He's been lying so long his organs have shifted and the vertical position makes him nauseous and dizzy. Dave, can you make the Ballantine beer circle with your thumb and forefinger? A boy your age must like beer."

His eyes blinked once.

"Watch me. Come on—try."

Minutes ticked away as he concentrated on trying. The therapist firmly grabbed his right arm and fist that was locked to his chin and pulled down. Her action triggered my panic button.

"Is it possible you could break his arm?"

"I'd better not! I know it seems cruel but it's the only way to get it down. The tendons are locked at the elbow. Later we'll use the ice treatment." She worked each knuckle and joint from his head to his toes. Ordered a neck collar too. Up to this time there had been much discussion about one, but nothing was finalized. Everything she said and did impressed me.

The speech assistant fed David lunch. My father and I observed. She was a sweet, young thing with loose, shoulder-length brown hair and super-long frosted fingernails. Eating went slowly and when her time was up, I finished. She was hardly out the door when my father said, "Why in the world doesn't she tie that hair back and cut those fingernails? It's not even sanitary. If I were you, I'd tell her."

"Dad, I've already complained about the top speech therapist. The important thing is, she has a good rapport with David."

Immediately after lunch Judy, the occupational therapist, returned. "David, watch me." She picked up a round wooden block and dropped it into a round cutout hole. The block fell inside the square box she was holding. "Now, David, you put all these different-shaped blocks into the proper holes."

David didn't move a muscle. We waited. I marveled at her patience. She did not give directions again nor fuss about his just sitting there. She seemed to know he was thinking. After what seemed half an hour, his left hand moved in all directions before he was able to get it to the top of the box. All movements were painfully slow and difficult. He lifted the lid of the box and one by one threw the blocks inside. Unfortunately, she didn't seem to think it was as funny as I did. Could it be he considered colored balls and wooden blocks kid stuff? David, age two, sitting on the beat-up potty seat flashed into my mind. I had given his busy fingers a Playskool spool that had five round wooden rings shaped like a cone. Twenty minutes later when I flushed the toilet it overflowed. I called a plumber. Hours later, sweating and swearing, the plumber removed the toilet in desperation. Cradled in the china neck was the perfect-sized ring.

Now the team arrived to transport David to the afternoon session of physical therapy. I tagged along.

"Who are you?" asked the therapist.

"I'm his mother."

"Well, you're not allowed in here."

"The morning therapist let me watch."

"No one watches me!"

Hanging onto my self-confidence, I insisted. "But you don't understand. I'm writing David's story."

"Oh, really?" The door slammed shut in my face. My dignity injured, I went home.

The phone was ringing as I turned the key in the lock. It was the social worker from Overlook. She said she was sorry to have missed me and would I stop by her office on my return trip.

It was one of those "fooler fall days." Quickly I changed into a sleeveless summer dress, threw some laundry into the machine, dumped detergent on top, set the dial, and banged the door shut behind me. The bed would have to remain unmade. I kept asking myself, What does a social worker do and what could she possibly want of me?

"My service," she said, "is to help you now that David is on a full rehabilitation program. In his case he needs more intensified therapy than Overlook can give him. This is basically a medical hospital. The time has come for you to think about moving him to a rehabilitation institute."

Those were sweeping statements. I heard every word but inside was screaming, Wait a minute! The room grew hot. My face tightened and flushed as I confessed, "The thought never crossed my mind. I haven't even met the doctor of rehab here."

"He's only at the hospital two days a week and asked me to talk with you first. I'll arrange an appointment. Have you ever heard of Kessler Institute of Rehabilitation?"

"No."

"They do miraculous things."

"Where is it?"

"In West Orange. Here's a brochure to read at your leisure. Why don't I make an appointment for you to visit? Is morning or afternoon best?"

"Morning, but do I have to go right away?"

"I'd say as soon as possible. Kessler has a four- to six-week waiting list."

She made the appointment. I drifted out of her office like a sleepwalker, baffled. David was still seriously ill. For fifty-four days everyone was absorbed with fighting for his life; now suddenly they wanted to move him. It wasn't logical. I shelved the whole idea and went upstairs to feed David.

The family had already arrived. "Hey, David," Darryl said, "just what I've always wanted. A graham cracker dipped in applesauce. Open up. Ah, you don't want it? How about a wet noodle?"

Darryl, like all of us, had not lost his sense of humor. In feeding, the trick was to get the food into his mouth once it opened and your fingers out before it clamped shut. Otherwise you had swollen purple fingers for days. I knew. Liquids were impossible due to his delayed swallow. I was greatly relieved when our family doctor said, "Forget the fluids. He's getting enough with the supplementary tube feedings."

Music was still being played whenever possible. Always before leaving at night we'd set his tape recorder. I turned out to be Two Guys' best battery customer. The salesman finally asked, "What are you doing with all those batteries?" When I explained he said, "Keep these extras in the refrigerator; they'll last longer. I'll say a prayer for your boy tonight."

"Thanks," I smiled. It seemed incredible to me how many total strangers responded.

The phone was ringing, ringing, ringing. My sleepy eyes opened and moved to the clock on the table. It was midnight. Quickly I answered, "Hello."

"Mom, this is Greg."

"Greg, where are you?"

"At Lehigh."

"When did you get in?"

"Tonight. What's up? Some friends on campus told me Dave had a car accident and you've been looking for me."

"Come home and we'll tell you all about it."

My prayers had been answered. It had taken seven weeks, but Greg had been found.

He arrived the next day.

*   *   *

"Hey Dave, I'm Greg—your traveling brother. I've come home."

Without question David recognized him immediately, and although it was hard for him to respond, we all knew he was happy to see Greg and a little surprised. I don't think he realized until that moment that Greg hadn't been coming with us when we visited him.

The following morning after breakfast the physical therapist arrived with David's neck collar. "That's quite ingenious," I observed.

"OT made it. They poured a liquid plastic into a mold of David's neck and it came out like this— perforated, pliable, and lightweight. Let's see how it fits, David . . . Perfect."

It was contoured to fit under his chin and extend flat onto his upper chest and shoulder area. Immediately his left hand struggled to move toward it. I knew he hated it. As a toddler David could never stand his snowsuit zippered up to his neck. I left the room thinking "lots of luck," as the therapist was telling David its purpose and need. It was my day to visit Kessler Institute of Rehabilitation.

Kessler sits high on a hill in the middle of a lush, wooded area. The view is breathtaking. As I approached, the door automatically opened. Wheelchair patients were everywhere. I stared at leg stumps, stiff, uncomfortable-looking neck collars, and withered limbs covered with complicated braces. One patient, lying on his stomach, was strapped onto a stretcher. I had never seen so many handicapped people. It shook me. I swallowed a lump in my throat and gave a smile the width of a hair as a patient asked, "Would you pick up my cigarettes?" Quickly I retrieved them.

"Would you please light one and put it in my mouth?"

"Ah . . . I don't smoke, but I'll sure try."

The first match didn't strike. Just then the social director introduced herself and lit the cigarette. What a relief!

Kessler houses forty-eight patients plus countless

outpatients. The bedrooms are large, airy, and cheerful. They reminded me of Darryl's dorm at Cornell. The decor was pleasing and rooms had either two or four beds. We went through a large dining room and my guide told me that every patient ate there unless he was under bed rest by doctor's orders. It was not a hospital, and all patients were dressed and moving. I was not allowed in the individual therapy rooms, but had a peek through the door windows. I saw physical, occupational, speech, and hearing therapy, activities for daily-living training and other prevocational programs, plus psychological and educational services. The staff consisted of thirty-five professionals, and all patients received twenty-four-hour nursing care.

I left Kessler with mixed emotions. I remember saying to the social director, "But David is still very much a bed patient."

"From what you tell me, he should be here now. We like to get them as early as possible."

I didn't answer. I didn't know how to say, I'm not convinced. David's condition wasn't like any of those patients I had just seen. I didn't want to put him there all day and all night for who knew how long. Besides, there were no visiting hours during the day; what would he do? Confusion overwhelmed me.

As the car came to a stoplight I asked, "What do you think about all this, God?"

"Can he talk, walk, eat, or care for himself?"

And then the neurologist's words pounded through, "He has lost his entire motor control!"

I had no choice. Kessler would regain David's motor control for him. That was their business. They had proved it for thousands of patients. Why was I fighting it? In fact, why were tears running down my cheeks? Kessler was new hope.

That settled, the car gathered power and rushed homeward. My mind was racing. I had so much to do —reread the personal belongings listed for inpatients, go shopping, and sew those wretched little name tapes on his clothing. David would get a kick out of seeing "Darryl" tapes. That was all I had.

At noon the assistant speech therapist at Overlook came bouncing into the room with all ten fingers high in the air.

"Look, David. I cut my nails just for you." David appeared nonplussed, but Grandpa would be pleased.

On Friday the top speech therapist fed David lunch. The assistant and I observed. She insisted on talking about his brain damage in detail as she pushed the food. Her theory: Fill the mouth, otherwise he doesn't know it's there. When a spasm came she'd grab his head and chin in a wrestler's arm lock until it passed. I winced. She knew the spasm came from gas pains and would inform our family doctor. I felt she triggered them. Perhaps the social director was right. Kessler should get David as soon as possible.

Over the weekend we slipped David's best friend, Helmut, in to see him.

"Hey Dave, want a beer?"

His eyes blinked once. We pushed and encouraged, never letting up, always looking for more and more recall. Otherwise he would have been perfectly content to lie there and vegetate. One eye blink meant yes, two meant no.

Darryl and Barb had brought a plastic Snoopy dog, and when David moved his left hand to take it we were all thrilled. The nurses had given him a ten-cent-store cricket. Once he mastered it, it chirped and chirped and chirped, till one of us would yell, "That's enough!" He also could get his hairbrush up to his head—never mind brushing it; just the act was enough. Again and again he pulled on the neck collar. It annoyed him and I could see his neck was red from its pressure. First I lined it with soft cotton. That proved to be dumb; the cotton got hot and stuck to his neck. Next I lined it with the cure-all, moleskin. Not one wrinkle either —but for David, no way. One day a volunteer returned him from therapy and left him sitting outside his room in the wheelchair. Alone, idle, and unhappy, he pulled and pulled until the collar ripped and fell to the floor. I was outwardly furious, but secretly elated. It was a flash of the old David. It reminded me of the day he took his first swimming lesson. He stood at the edge of the community pool, sneezed, jumped in, came up, sneezed again, jumped in, came up, sneezed, jumped in. On and on it went. Grandma and I sat at the pool edge discussing his allergy, how cold it was, and perhaps we were starting him too soon. At the end of the half-hour I decided, "David, let's forget swimming. You're allergic to the chlorine."

"No, I'm coming back tomorrow." He was determined. Recently, he had been on the high school swim team until his allergy caused repeated eye infections.

His left hand continued to develop strength and follow commands. Time and again he would partially pull out the nose tube. I cringed as I saw the nurses shove it back all stuck with goop.

"Couldn't you clean it off first?" I asked.

"Never! That would be asking for an infection." I questioned that with a frown. Each time he pulled it out farther and each time it was pushed back and plastered with more adhesive tape.

"David, don't fight it," I reasoned. "It's got to stay until you can swallow food."

The following day the nurse greeted me with, "David pulled out his nose tube today."

"I don't blame him," I replied. "He's had it for forty days."

"The doctor's with him now. He says it must go back."

"Doctor, please leave it out. I'm sure I can get enough food into him."

"I'll give you twenty-four hours and no more. He's lost over forty pounds already." The neurologist had spoken again.

I rushed right home and made my gourmet Burgundy meatballs, special beef stew, and all the foods

David loved. He ate. All it took was time, and my time was his time.

Are you wondering where all the friends were who stood by us during those tense days in ICU? They were still with us one hundred percent. Now that I think about it, it's unbelievable. Candles were burning and more being lit. Prayer circles widened. The psychic group healings continued.

Others offered, "If John and you are up to it, come after visiting hours. We'll have a relaxed dinner, maybe a few hands of bridge. Be good for you to have a change of atmosphere."

The new assistant chaplain saw me daily. Now he asked, "Will you be able to give up David to Kessler?"

"I know he needs professional help and I can't give it."

"What will you do during the day?"

"Pick up some of my old activities." But when we parted there was a lump in my throat. It wouldn't be easy. He knew it and I knew it.

I don't know about you, but I hate to run my car through the inspection station lineup. Consequently, I procrastinate. It was September 27—the last inspection day of the month. I hurried down the corridor after giving David breakfast, determined to go right that minute, when our family doctor caught me.

"I have good news. We're transferring David to a private room tomorrow."

"Why?" I was shocked.

"His case is no longer serious."

"But he's only been in Special Care for sixteen days. He still needs close supervision."

"He has to go off the ninth floor. He's been on it for a total of seventy days."

"I don't want a private room. How will they know if he needs something? He can't talk or ring the buzzer."

"They don't have a semiprivate room."

"Then wait for one." I was really getting annoyed.

"Will you stop worrying! He's the pet of the hospital. He'll have as much attention as he's getting here. I've already spoken to the nurses. Smile. It's progress, and visiting hours are 11 A.M. to 8:30 P.M."

He left me standing in the middle of the corridor. The decision had been made. I wasn't one bit happy. I knew David would never get the attention and care he was receiving on the ninth floor. Private nurses—that was the answer. On second thought, how could we possibly afford three shifts a day? I felt sick. In desperation I turned to God. "What do you think?"

"Would your family doctor move him if he wasn't ready?"

Thanks were due to those who nursed and worked with David. Often, when free, nurses would spend time talking to him. Linda in particular had stayed beyond hours to learn from the neurologist how she could further help David. And I will never forget Danny, a young inhalation therapist, filled with compassion. Several times a day he gave David therapy in ICU and now in Special Care. Many nights he'd pop in while we were there to say, "David, I'll be back later and we'll talk." I was so grateful for all who really became involved. To merely say "thank you" was inadequate. I repeated my custom: a cheesecake, and David's fudge—this time done to perfection.

PRIVATE ROOM

September 28, 1972. Condition satisfactory.

Room 515 was next to the nurses' station on the street level. That was a plus—no more riding elevators —but the size was a minus. It looked like a walk-in closet with wall TV. But then, remembering the hospital director was only charging us a semiprivate rate, I hated myself for being critical.

After breakfast we had our "therapy time."

"David, take a deep breath and blow this feather."

I held it close to his mouth but it didn't move a fraction.

"Tomorrow's another day. We're not the type to give up, right?"

His eyes blinked once.

"Look—I found this whistle in your bureau drawer. Did Bill, the lifeguard at Clover Hill, give it to you on closing day?"

He blinked once.

"I thought so. Take a deep breath and exhale.

"I'll get a plastic one. They blow easier. One more try. Blow out the birthday candle."

Excitedly I lit the candle and held it close, almost too close, and let it burn down to my fingers. The flame never flickered.

"David, believe me, one day you'll do all three things. Mouth exercise time."

I puckered. He almost puckered. "Move your tongue up, to the left, to the right, stick it out. That's better than yesterday. Close and swallow. Good." When the OT therapist came I read her facial expression as, "A mother playing therapist!"

My schedule really hadn't changed. I'd be back for lunch and depending on my mood, the weather, and David's routine, I'd stay at the hospital or go to a friend's house for the afternoon.

Suddenly I became very money-conscious (even if it wasn't my own). In the beginning the thought never occurred to me. We who waited in line to see our patients in ICU wore our feelings on the outside. We discussed everything; nothing was too personal. I recall the day a man standing in back of me asked, "Do you know what this unit costs a day?"

"I have no idea."

"I just found out today. It's one hundred and twenty dollars without medication, machines, or any extras."

My eyes popped wide open. In round numbers our expenses so far were enormous. "John says our hospitalization will cover, but that's a lot of money."

"Don't worry," he said. "I'm gonna tell all my wife's doctors—fall in line and when your turn comes, you'll get paid."

"Good idea."

Now I searched for street parking. The paid lot was swallowing three quarters a day. Police cars were constantly cruising the area, and parked cars were often ticketed or had a big chalk X on their tire. For this reason I was extra cautious about over-extending the two-hour limit. But my day came. There stood the fuzz

(David's word) writing a ticket. Switching to a fast run and waving my hand I called, "That's my car! I'm coming."

"Sorry, lady, the ticket's already written."

Checking my watch, I gasped, "But I'm only five minutes late."

"We never give out tickets for less than ten minutes overtime," he snapped, stuffing it under the windshield wiper.

I was furious. Some time ago a guard, who recognized me as a regular and always asked, "How's the boy?" suggested I ask for slugs for the paid lot. Today I would ask.

"May I help you?" asked the girl behind the credit desk.

"Would you believe I just got a parking ticket for being five minutes overtime? The guard told me you give slugs to people in my situation; I come three times a day."

"Which guard told you that?"

"I don't know his name and I don't see him on duty now."

"Never heard of it. Sorry."

Funny how a lousy two-dollar ticket can get to you. Feeling picked on, I wrote a letter to the police chief and enclosed my check.

Three days later, all smiles, I hurried into David's room.

"Remember how mad I was about the parking ticket I got? I said I'd write a letter and I did. Today my check was returned with a letter of apology from the police chief. He said he has asked all his men to be more considerate in the hospital zone. How about that?"

There was no doubt in my mind that David understood and enjoyed the story even though he couldn't respond. When I was on one of my "it's-not-fair" causes he'd say, "Write one of your famous letters, Mom."

Every day the speech assistant fed him lunch, and

when her time was up, I finished. Feeding was pro-
gressing. Maybe that was because we were all learning
—David, the therapists, and myself. By now he could
guide small pieces of finger food with his left hand
into his mouth. The liquid-protein diet, previously giv-
en through the nose tube, he now drank from a cup.
He would eat about one third of the prepared meal,
which took between forty and fifty minutes. I recorded
all food and liquid intake on the wall chart. When I
saw a banana lying on our kitchen table the idea
struck me that it would be good for David.

"Know what this is?" I asked, holding up the
banana.

His eyes blinked once. I peeled about half and
handed it to him. With his left hand he moved it
toward his mouth. I should have known better—when
did David ever take a small bite of anything? I flew
out the door, screaming at the top of my lungs, "David's
choking, David's choking!"

Three nurses ran in. They tugged and pulled him
into a sitting position—David had no trunk control—
and the banana slid down. "You okay, David?" they
asked. He blinked.

"I have never felt so dumb," I mumbled.

"Relax, it's all over."

September 29. I met with the doctor of rehabilitation.

"Mrs. Landvater, I want to assure you I have spoken
to all the therapists about what they say in front
of David. I know this has bothered you and I agree,
he understands a great deal."

"Thank you. I've only been unhappy with the top
speech therapist."

"Sometimes," he volunteered, "she goes into more
detail than is necessary."

"Doctor, what would you say is David's prognosis?"

"Well, I believe he will regain his motor control.
He'll walk again, perhaps dragging his right leg. But

he's young and I like to think after Kessler gets his right arm down he'll regain its use too. I've seen it happen time and time again. When a person is as devoted as you are it's amazing what can be accomplished. Next week he'll be on a full exercise program here. That includes mat and transfer activities, standing and sitting balance."

"I thought I would keep him here another month."

"That's realistic. He's a challenge to me and I'd like to work with him a little longer."

I left his office wishing he were available every day. What a pity a hospital of this size didn't have a full-time rehab doctor. Walking to David's room, my mind had not only accepted Kessler, but was looking forward to it.

The patient diagonally across the hall from David was a nun. She remained in solitude with her door open only a crack. Today she stuck her head out and gestured for me to come over.

"I see you and your lovely family coming and going," she said. "What is wrong with the girl?"

"The girl is our seventeen-year-old son, David. He had a car accident."

"Oh, saints above, with the hair he looked like a girl. I'll include him in my prayers."

The following day she motioned again. "Put this under his pillow tonight," she said. "I have been in prayer for him constantly." She handed me a printed prayer card. Later that night David's friends were standing around his bed. He was catnapping. Kim picked up the card the sister had given me. "What is this?" she asked. I explained.

"Why don't we pass it around, and each of you give your own prayer for David? Then I'll put it underneath his pillow."

Some bowed their heads, some touched David, some looked up, some stepped back. *"Where two or three are gathered together in my name, there am I in their midst,"* flashed before me, and I knew God had heard our pleas.

The following day I held up a shiny red apple.

"David, know what this is?"

His eyes blinked once.

"Know what to do with it?"

He took it with his left hand and put it to his mouth. Quickly and firmly I stopped his hand. "Take a small bite—I don't want you to choke. Remember it has a core."

He took a small bite, chewed, and swallowed. He ate the whole apple.

The next day when our family doctor arrived, I proudly said, "Watch this." I handed the apple to David.

"Very good, David," he exclaimed. "What will your mother think of next?"

From then on he had one a day. The third day he choked. The thought had never occurred to me before, but now it was clear: A piece of apple stuck in his throat was not like a soft banana. Two floor nurses were getting nowhere. The head nurse was called. She gave him water—tons of it, which created a sudsy foam.

"I think we should call a doctor," I suggested.

"What would he do?" asked the head nurse.

"Well, my gosh, he ought to know more than we do."

Minutes passed. All the while David was bright red, coughing and gagging. Finally an inhalation therapist arrived. No one knew exactly what to do, but all agreed—no more water. I was frantic! Ten minutes had passed.

"We just can't stand here and let the boy choke to death. Call a doctor!"

"He's still breathing. Why don't you step outside. You're getting upset."

I dashed down the hall to the pay phone and called our family doctor. His nurse answered. I explained the problem. "Mrs. Landvater, he's in the hospital.

They'll handle it. Just relax." Slamming the phone back on its hook, I thought, This isn't possible. This really isn't happening.

"God, you wouldn't let him choke to death on an apple, would you?"

Go back to his room.

One lonely nurse remained. "The apple went down," she said.

Relief flooded over me. "What's that funny noise he's making?"

"He's crying. Might have been the best thing for him—loosened things up. I'd stick to sherbet and soft things tonight. His throat must be raw."

"Good idea—I'm through trying any more brilliant ideas."

For months, day in and day out, I had been motivating David for some verbal response. Maybe the nurse had a point—if the choking caused him to cry, perhaps he could laugh.

"David, must I tickle you to make you laugh?"

He blinked his eyes once.

"Okay, here goes." My fingers danced at the old vulnerable spot—the ribs.

David laughed out loud.

Gloriously happy, I ran to the nurses' station. "David laughed. He did. He really laughed."

The speech and OT therapist had made David a wooden talk board. It was designed to fit as a lapboard over his wheelchair in the front with a cut-out for his body. Colored tiles had been glued on and underneath were the words *bad, good, mother, hurt, toilet, food, yes, no.* I read the words and David pointed to them with his left hand. He understood them all. I was never satisfied once he mastered something. I added more words written on pieces of adhesive tape. And each day he was anxious to show the family what new thing he could do.

A few days later Kay, a nurse from ICU, walked in. I remember the first time she was on duty after David was brought in. I recognized her as a member of our church. Instantly our relationship was cemented. During those tense, fearful days it was Kay who wrapped her strong, big arm around me time and again with a word of hope. It was Kay who told me her own son had been in a coma from a car accident and now was fine. It was Kay who, in a thousand ways, made David more comfortable and constantly tried to trigger a response. Kay washed his hair the first time. Kay helped him out in the chair the first time. Kay fed him his first soft-cooked egg. Kay stood by when the trach was removed, waiting for his first word. Kay had pushed him down the hall to Special Care. Now she stood at the foot of his bed.

"David, let's see you move that left arm—out to the side, up, down. Very good. Now the leg. Tremendous! You couldn't do that when you were in ICU. What about this right leg?" She touched it, then gave the command, "Move it." He had never moved it. She knew it and I knew it. Our eyes met, then moved to David. His whole body tensed, the left leg moved, and then the right leg moved. Only a fraction, but we saw it.

"You're going to be okay, David. Keep working."

After she left, the father of David's friend John came for the first time. He stood at the foot of David's bed, towering six feet tall and weighing close to two hundred pounds. David had spent a week with his family at the shore and called him the Big Bear.

"David," he yelled, "do you know who I am? Do you? Am I the Big Bear?"

David blinked his eyes once and then, for the first time, tried to talk. A vocal gibberish came out, but what a thrill!

On Friday the top speech therapist arrived.

"May I see you in the hall?" I asked.

"David's doing so well with his eating, it's really no longer a problem. I'd like to see you move on to other things. Your assistant suggested I bring pictures for recall. I've been using the *National Geographic* magazine."

"Mrs. Landvater, I don't think you understand the extent of David's brain damage." She continued throwing out medical terms and ended up with, "In cases this bad there isn't much else we can do."

My fiery eyes bore into hers. "How do you know unless you try?"

"I'm being realistic. I've spoken with David's neurologist and the brain damage is extensive."

"Don't stand there and tell me about David's brain damage. I have lived through these months of nothing but 'he doesn't hear, he doesn't see, he doesn't understand, he's not going to live.' He is alive. He does hear. He does see and he does understand. At least try the next step." I spun around and marched back into David's room, boiling mad.

The following day, while Barb was feeding David lunch, the top speech therapist returned. "I know your mother-in-law doesn't like me to talk about David's brain damage in front of him, but David understands he has brain damage."

That did it! The minute Barb told me I ran to the social worker.

"I don't want that speech therapist to see or ever work with David again. Out! She is finished! If she lives to be a hundred she'll never change her attitude. I will only accept her assistant. Please tell the doctor of rehabilitation."

Three months after David's accident he was drinking fluids through a straw. And he could change the TV channel by pushing the remote control button. As a matter of fact, he ran the cycle over and over. Every night at 5 P.M. he and I watched "The Flintstones." More and more of his personality was returning. I didn't know how much until Father Ashe entered.

"I saw David this morning in PT," he said.

"Oh really? How was he doing?"

Father stood at the foot of David's bed, staring

straight at him. "He was being stubborn, weren't you, David?"

David didn't move a muscle. Neither did Father Ashe.

"David, listen to me. Very few people are ever asked to go through what you are. This is the most difficult challenge you will ever have to face, but I know you can accept it. Tomorrow I want to see you cooperating."

The next day he returned. "David, I was very proud of you this morning. I'll tell you what. When you can say 'cold beer' I'll bring you one. Is that a deal?"

His eyes blinked once.

David had known Father since Cub Scout days. More recently, he had joined skiers to the slopes on a bus trip Father had arranged. I remembered the first time he came to see David. Lance and I stood by David's bed in ICU as Father offered a beautiful prayer. Later, in the hall, he said, "If God should take him from you, you must remember he has given David to you to love and enjoy for seventeen full years."

My eyes filled with tears. I couldn't speak. I listened, I heard, I understood, but I couldn't accept that possibility.

At the time of David's accident he was wearing his wire-rimmed glasses. It was incredible, but when Mr. Weber (the owner of the property where the crash occurred) pried the car door open with a crowbar, there sat David with both seat belts buckled and his glasses intact. Now Dr. Romas, our family eye doctor, came to Overlook Hospital to give David an examination. It was surprising how intelligently David responded to the examination by blinking his eyes. The doctor determined he had sight in both eyes, the right one being extremely weak. "He has nerve damage in back of the optical nerve," he said. "This causes double vision, nystagmus, a jump in the eyes, and hinders his peripheral range. It's all a result of the brain-stem concussion."

Another unglowing report, but I wasn't upset. I rationalized, "It's only part of his motor control. It will return."

Time.

As long as David remained at Overlook, people called to ask his condition. I will never forget how friends surrounded me with their strength. Almost every day one arrived during lunch to hold his wobbly head while I fed him. Luella continued to come daily. One morning she rushed in carrying a wicker basket.

"David, this morning you and I are going to eat breakfast together. I made Roman meal and it's going to give you new energy. This cereal was eaten by the Roman legionnaires. It made them so strong they conquered the world. That's a true story. It says so right here on this box."

David was really impressed. He ate every bite, to my surprise. At home he'd never eat cooked cereal—he called it chuck-up food.

His school friends came regularly with something to promote recall. Gary brought his guitar. "Dave, see if you can pick out a chord.

"That's terrific! It's the G chord."

David had just bought a guitar and with Gary's help was struggling to play it.

Red letter day—October 27. The social worker bounced into David's room at noontime, all excited.

"Kessler has a bed for David on Monday. You're to arrive at 11 A.M. I'll make the necessary arrangements with your local ambulance."

"That's perfect timing," I said. "Our one hundred and twenty days' coverage runs out next week. Thanks for all you've done."

I'd been preparing David for the past five weeks for his move to Kessler, and now that the time had come, he seemed to take it in stride.

Sunday I attended chapel services for the last time. I will never forget the chaplain's words, "This morning

I want to pray for two people in particular. David, a young boy who has been seriously ill for a long time and now is going to a rehabilitation institute, and his mother. She has shown us here at Overlook a faith we did not have."

October 30—moving day. While David and I were waiting for the ambulance, the sister across the hall came in. She took off her big gold cross and pressed it to David's head. He understood her blessing and blinked to tell her.

After she left Judy, the OT therapist, walked in.

"The nurses said they had already given you David's pill bag. Would you please put this with it?"

She handed me a white business envelope. As I was about to drop it into the bag, I noticed it wasn't sealed. I opened it.

"Since September 6 we have given David range-of-motion exercises to all four extremities, daily. In October he was put on a full exercise program including mat and transfer activities, standing, and sitting balance. Heel cords have been stretched daily. He has severe elbow flexion contraction and shows no voluntary motion. Lately he has become resistive to treatment." It was signed, "PT Department."

My stomach tightened. I reread—"shows no voluntary motion." That wasn't good. The second report was from Judy, the OT therapist. Words began to jump out at me.

"David has a very domineering, determined, and anxious mother who very cleverly can manipulate the therapist, and she talks to him as if he were a child."

My blood pressure soared! How dare she! Was this the price I had to pay for firing the speech therapist? If I gave this report to Kessler, I would bear the stamped label "problem mother." I sat glued to the chair, holding a hot report. My heart was pounding dangerously. "Don't panic," I said to myself. "Nothing is insurmountable." I could destroy it. Who would know? My eyes turned to David. It was really unimportant what anyone thought about me. David was all that mattered.

I got up and dropped the envelope into the pill bag.

The door opened. The rescue workers had arrived. Two nurses assisted as they lifted David onto the narrow ambulance stretcher.

"See you at Kessler, David. Don't forget to check out the ambulance. It's your first Cadillac ride."

His eyes blinked, but I could feel his fear.

I walked to the business office. "David Landvater is being discharged today."

"Just a moment," she said in a tone indicating, "don't you dare leave until I give permission." The minutes ticked by slowly. I grew nervous. After one hundred and fifteen days our bill must be unreal. She checked one file, then another; moved to a file in the corner, pulled out a drawer, read a card, closed the drawer, and faced me.

With a straight face she simply said, "You are free to go."

"Just like that?"

"Your hospitalization will cover."

My hands pushed the exit door, recalling the night of David's accident. "You wouldn't take my seventeen-year-old boy, would you, God?"

Three and a half months later we were leaving Overlook Hospital.

Time.

PART TWO

Kessler Institute

The year—1972. The month—November. The time—11 A.M. The weather—sunny and crisp.

John and I met at Kessler Institute to admit David. Married almost twenty-five years, with four sons aged 24, 23, 22 and 17, we had never seen one of them inside an ambulance before. I shivered as the flashing light came up the hill.

Rushing to David, I asked, "Did you like your Cadillac ride?"

He blinked and, for the first time, broke into a smile. A "first" always gave me a wonderful feeling deep down inside. Today I considered it a good omen.

The receptionist directed the rescue squad volunteers to Room 168. John and I followed. A nurse was waiting.

"David, at Kessler we use a first-name basis. I'm Bim. We'll soon get to know each other. And you're his parents?"

We nodded.

"First I'll change his catheter. We don't use this kind at Kessler."

She discarded it like the plague itself. With one swift hand movement she coiled the tube in a circle on the edge of the bed that led down to the drain bag. "That's so he doesn't have any pull or strain," she explained.

Very impressed, I hastened to add, "I sure wish we had known that trick. David kept pulling on the tube. I thought it bothered him."

"Probably did. Now David, we'll take your temperature."

John cut in, "Dave always has it taken rectally."

"At Kessler we do it orally." Her steel eyes met mine.

"David won't bite it," I said very slowly and distinctly. "I've prepared him."

Still and all I prayed, "Please God, don't let him bite it."

"Have you met with the social service director?" she asked.

"No."

"Why don't you go to her office now and then wait in the outer lobby. Our internist will check David, then will want to see you both."

I had the feeling she wanted to be rid of us. We left after we saw the thermometer safely out of David's mouth.

At first sight I liked the social service director. She seemed genuinely interested in our David. I relaxed.

"Tell me about David before his accident. What year was he in high school?"

"He would have been a senior in September."

"What kind of student was he?"

"Average to good. Mostly B's with an A in music."

"Was he active in sports?"

"He was on the swim team, did some track running, and worked on the high bar in gymnastics. Played the drums in the band, too."

"Have any hobbies?"

"Photography was his latest. He had taken and developed some pictures for the school."

"What was his personality before the accident?"

"Well, to quote his teachers, he's a happy, well-adjusted boy. Seems I'm answering everything good. Hope you don't think we have one of those 'perfect sons.' "

"I'm sure you're being honest. You see we want to restore David to what he was in every way."

Boy, I thought, her attitude is terrific. She directed a few questions to John concerning insurance and then we waited in the lobby. Lunchtime passed. We were hungry but afraid to leave. At 2 P.M. the internist called us.

"I have examined your son," he said. "In brain-damage cases such as his, patients are very unpredictable." His bright blue, calculating eyes held mine. "Has he ever responded to you?"

"Oh yes."

"In what way?"

"He blinks once for yes, twice for no, and can follow commands. He really understands most of what anyone says."

"I didn't get any response. None at all." His words hung like poisoned fruit. Before I had a chance to get my thoughts together to answers, he stood and moved toward the door.

"We'll begin our evaluation and set up a schedule tomorrow." Throwing a glance my way, he continued, "Since we're not a general hospital, it would be best if you didn't contact me for a month."

A month! my mind screamed. My mouth opened but nothing came out; the internist was shaking hands with John, and I knew our conference had ended. John went back to work and I went home.

Since the accident I hadn't touched a thing in David's room. I had an obsession about leaving everything as David had kept it. Now I went in to pack his clothes.

My eyes swept the room like a tower beacon. Time turned back.

David was loading his five-piece drum set plus a stool and a rolled remnant of carpet (I could never understand why he needed it) into the trunk of my car. What spilled over he piled onto the back seat. We took off to the jam session like sardines packed in a can. I did it because it was my motherly duty. How I wished I could do it now. Hanging from the ceiling above his desk was a homemade sand candle. That too brought back memories:

"David, I'm telling you this is the last stop. If the drugstore doesn't have the oil of cinnamon, too bad." They had it.

On the wall he had attached an old water spigot. One day I showed it to a friend interested in antiques. She turned the knob and liquid ran out. Puzzled, I shoved open the sliding closet door and saw our old picnic jug. A hose was attached, leading to the spigot. With my voice unevenly rising I yelled, "It's apple wine. The little devil!"

On his bed were the new orange and yellow love-flower sheets, still in their package. David had picked them to match his yellow walls. They arrived the day after his accident. Ripping open the plastic, I put them on the bed. He would be pleased. Kessler was definitely going to return David as he was before his accident. Of this I was positive. I tossed a rummage sale suitcase onto the bed. Decisions, decisions . . . should I take his sandals, shoe boots, or the black tie shoes he hated? I took all three, along with his khakis—or "old man pants" as Kim called them—and the new underwear. One thing a mother cannot do is send her boy away in ratty gray shorts.

It was 5:45 P.M. when I returned to Kessler. The receptionist icily announced, "Visiting hours are 6 P.M. to 8:30 P.M." My bright smile evaporated.

"Well," I admitted, "I didn't know how long it would take with traffic and all."

She smiled, and then I knew we'd be friends. David's brother, Darryl, was feeding him in bed. Looking around, I saw three roommates. A young boy about David's age called from the corner, "Would you hand me my water pitcher?"

"Be glad to." He gulped all the water.

"Do you always drink that much water?"

"We have to drink lots of fluids, especially cranberry juice. Better tell David."

I had a million and one questions. What does cranberry juice do? How long have you been here? What happened to you? I asked none.

"Mrs. Landvater?"

I turned to see Jim wheeling toward David.

"Hi, Jim."

"I thought you'd like to know a fellow named Danny came to see Dave today around 3 P.M. Dave seemed to know him."

"That was the inhalation therapist at Overlook. He promised David he'd come. What a guy."

"Tomorrow between my therapy I'll check in on Dave. See if he needs anything."

"Thanks. Just knowing you're here makes us feel better."

John and I knew Jim's parents through our church. Jim was a student in forestry when he fell and broke his neck. Other patients stopped in. Jack, a double amputee, explained that he had gotten caught in a cement mixer, and then looking at David, he said, "I feel so sorry for him. Must be awful not to be able to talk."

John was shocked to see one of his sailing buddies who had a stroke while visiting his native Germany. Our two-and-a-half hours flew by. My heart sank. There was a look in David's eyes—not exactly fear, but more questioning. Why did you bring me here? What's going to happen to me? I hated to leave. However, his short-term memory had been badly affected and he'd soon forget what he was questioning. This was due to the initial damage of the brain stem knocking out his motor control. Right now it was a blessing. Darryl and John set up the stereo, speakers, and earphones, hoping they would help him cope with his new surroundings. At home he always nodded out with his music.

The second night I pinched myself. I couldn't believe what I saw. David was being wheeled from the dining room. Not only had he eaten with the other patients, but he was fully dressed. Do you associate dressing with recovery? I do. He looked utterly exhausted but happy in his old-man pants (now ten sizes too big). His schedule was attached to the wheelchair. Speech—9:30 to 10 A.M. Physical therapy—10 to 11 A.M. Activities for daily living—11:30 to 12 noon. Lunch. Occupational therapy—1 to 2 P.M. Physical therapy—2 to 3 P.M. What a schedule! Recalling the neurologist's words, "David needs total rehabilitation,"—I accepted it without dispute. Two orderlies took David to his room. One grabbed him underneath the arms, the other held both pant cuffs together with one hand and his belt with the other hand. On the count of three they lifted him straight up and over onto the bed. It was a slick transfer. The curtains closed. They were getting him ready for bed. Everybody talked to David as though they expected him to answer at any minute. Their attitude was very positive.

Saturday I marched in with the family Roll-o-Dice game. Placing dice in his left hand and the game box on the tray table, I said, "Drop the dice, David."

In time the left hand released them. "You got six, what are you gonna do?"

At moments like this I really got up-tight. I desperately wanted David to point to the number, but it was such a slow, difficult task that I wanted to do it for him. Eventually his left hand touched block number six. I smiled, happy as a lark.

The next game I didn't call the dice total. David

totaled it. The object was to clear the board, turning no more than two blocks at one throw. He had total recall of the game.

Sunday Lance brought a new Etch-a-Sketch. David knew exactly what to do with it. Again and again his left hand missed the knob. Medically, he had ataxia—his hand wouldn't go where he wanted it to go. Determined, he finally grasped the knob, but it wouldn't turn. Silently I shouted, "Hell, knob, turn!"

"David," I warned, "you're pushing down instead of turning."

While we fought for self-control, he got one short weak line. Delighted, I rushed on, "Each day we'll keep working and soon you'll be making lines all over the board."

Weekends at Kessler are quiet and long. Most patients go home. Visiting hours are 1 to 8:30 P.M. We ate in the staff dining room while David had his dinner with the other patients. This turned out to be therapy time for families. Each told their story. We were surrounded by tragic experiences, and somehow theirs seemed worse than ours. Lennie, a young family man, was driving a snowplow on the thruway when he stopped to lend assistance to a car in distress. As he was walking to the car, another car hit him. One leg had been amputated. The other had been operated on twice; soon he'd leave Kessler for the third operation on the good leg. In a few months he'd return for further rehabilitation.

Nurse Betty was a gem. She kept us posted daily. "David fell asleep in physical therapy today. His schedule has been changed."

Amazing! Here they adjusted their schedule to David. Monday, Wednesday, and Friday nights were shower and suppository nights. Like at Overlook, patients had no secrets. The orderlies took David into the shower room on a stretcher. During these breaks, families hung around the coffee machine in the hall and discussed progress.

After one week at Kessler, David appeared happy and content. He laughed, but only when a laugh was required, and could swallow pills. Another step of progress. However, the eighth night I panicked.

"David, how did you break your arm?" His right arm was in a huge plaster cast.

Betty explained, "The cast is to straighten it." (The right arm was still locked to his chin as a result of the initial injury.) "Tomorrow they'll open the cast at the elbow and crank the arm lower. He'll only have it on about three to four days."

"Remarkable! I'm sure glad we brought him here."

The following day his right elbow was swollen and the cast removed. It hadn't been fully successful, but they would try again. Excitedly, Betty told us, "Dave picked out his name on the typewriter with his left hand in occupational therapy today." Of course I knew he knew his own name, but now they knew too. As for the neck collars, he'd run through three different types. Many clever ideas had been executed but all had failed. "He won't keep it on," was the cry.

The internist retorted, "David, if you won't wear it, then hold your head up yourself. Do you understand?"

The head went up, but soon dropped. Immediately the patients picked up the chant, "David, get that head up. David, get that head up. David, get that head up and keep it up."

We all racked our brains for clever ideas to stimulate his mind. Darryl and John thought of blackjack poker. They dealt the cards on the tray table and doled out the pennies. David shoved his betting money to the center and slid the cards over the table edge with his left hand. It ruined the cards, but who cared? He had full recall, and when our minister came, he eagerly took David on. The first game Dean won, but the second David won fair and square. At this point he was able to give more facial expression—the left side responding more than the right—and he let us know he played to win.

The annoying catheter was removed a week later. He had worn it for four months. A "Texas" sheath (its trade name) was literally glued on, with a catch bag strapped to his leg. David looked upon it all with a weak smile. John shrugged, "Dave, leg bags at Kessler are like tracheotomies in ICU—everyone has one." But when I learned that every two to three days they used a solvent to remove the glue when changing it, I understood the weak smile.

My days at home were falling into a more normal pattern since Kessler had no daytime visiting. At Overlook I had begun writing a play for the Woman's Club. It was finished and we began rehearsals. For the past nine years I'd had a part-time job as a professional book reviewer. My agent had previous contracts from various clubs and organizations and I fulfilled them. To be on stage again was my therapy. And our friends remained forever faithful. Many came to Kessler. I don't think our neighbors Heine and Frank ever missed a weekend. David's friends came too, which was even more important.

Lance had returned to college for his senior year. Greg was living in Bethlehem, Pennsylvania, but Darryl and Barb were nearby. My heart bled for those two. Their time was divided, stretched, and torn between work, themselves, and David. They had only been married seventeen months.

The day before Thanksgiving, David was given a left-handed wheelchair to promote independence. He was so pleased to show us what he could do, but after three turns he gave a centuries-old sigh and sat back as if to say, "That's all, folks!" As for Thanksgiving, we spent it at Kessler. The families were invited to have dessert with their patients. Grandpa, Darryl, Barb, Greg, and Lance joined us. I wasn't one bit upset—just grateful David was here; surely by Christmas he'd be home, at least for the day.

The following Saturday, nurse Betty reported, "David's in bed. He slid out of his wheelchair onto the floor. The internist examined him and didn't find anything, but felt we should observe him."

My ESP was coming through loud and clear. "David, I sure hope you didn't slide out on purpose, 'cause you could hurt yourself. This chair is a temporary thing. Do you understand that?"

He nodded. But the next day he slid out again. After the third time, the doctors and therapists got their heads together and decided the chair didn't feel right to David. They gave him another and the problem resolved itself. Again, I was impressed.

December first I ripped the calendar page off with vigor. It was my day to call the internist.

"Doctor, this is David's mother."

"Oh, yes."

"How do you find David? He's been at Kessler a month now."

"What can I say?" (pause)

"I'd hoped something good. To us, he seems more alert."

"Yes, he's more alert." (pause) "That's about all I can say at this time."

I hung up. Sick. Disappointed. Doctors! What was it the woman told me at Overlook? "Specialists don't give hope, only facts."

Time.

The next two weeks dragged. We continued to drive ourselves to spend every available minute with David. In a sense we felt cheated never seeing a doctor, but Kessler had routine family meetings every two weeks. John and I attended the first one together.

"What are your plans now that you have a handicapped?" asked the social service director.

I didn't have any. I didn't answer. John said, "I think your question is premature. It's not been determined if Dave will have any permanent handicap."

A short silence hung heavy, then she turned to the next family seated around the table. Listening to how others were coping with their individual problems, I sensed we had much to learn. From then on I attended whenever possible and found the sessions invaluable.

After David had been at Kessler for six weeks, I called for a conference with Dr. Sullivan, the medical director. An appointment was made within days. I waited in the lobby, feeling very shaky. It's the not knowing that triggers panic. With a warm, effortless smile the doctor walked toward me. All my shakiness vanished.

"Mrs. Landvater?"

"Yes."

"David is doing well."

It was love at first hearing. "You know," I replied, "I've never heard those words before."

"I'm sure you haven't and it's time you did." We walked into his office. During our conference he commented, "If we're lucky, David will walk out of here." Along with the cold hard facts, he was the first to give me hope.

"Can David come home for Christmas?"

"I rather doubt it. Actually, he won't miss Christmas this year."

No way could he convince me, but I didn't say so.

December 17, David came down with a virus. The next day the real problem revealed itself—a bowel blockage. He had hardly recovered from that when he began choking while we were visiting. Orderlies and nurses rushed in. Their voices were reassuring as they hung his head over the side of the bed.

"Easy, David, just spit it out."

That over, they uprighted him. He choked again. After the third session the doctor was called. David had a mucus plug. All this was really a part of the bowel blockage. They moved his bed next to the nurses' station. I cannot stress too strongly the compassion these people had for David, and for me, too. We had all experienced several tense days, and as I left they said, "Feel free to call in later if you're worried. We don't want you to lose any sleep." After five days, improvement was slight. The medication was changed and then he began to progress. But Dr. Sullivan had made his decision. "David may not go home for Christmas."

It was Christmas Eve and I was miserable. David was miserable too. I left his room about 8:15 P.M., ambling down the hall with head and feet and heart dragging, when a voice brought me up tall.

"Hi, Mom. How's Dave?"

It was our son Greg. My first words were unspoken. *Thank you, God.* David was so happy to see Greg that the nurses let him stay until midnight.

Christmas Day my two brothers and their families arrived from Pennsylvania with Grandpa. We ran a taxi service in shifts to Kessler. It was my day to be cook in the kitchen but when they headed home, I headed to Kessler. David was in bed, utterly exhausted. Now I understood the doctor's decision. In my mind this Christmas was already over. Looking ahead to next year, I knew things would be different. David would be home.

Another week passed. David's schedule was changed. Speech was crossed out because he was too frustrated about not being able to talk. He could do all the mouth exercises and make the various sound effects, but the consensus was that something had to trigger speech.

"Maybe," I said, "if David saw his cat, that would do it."

Animals are not allowed, but sometimes Kessler has elastic rules. Lance arrived with nervous Herbert on a leash. She had never worn one in all her five years and she hates cars. The minute Lance freed her, she slid underneath the heat vent. Frank, the guard, grinned.

"When the heat goes on she'll come out like a streak."
We waited and waited while beautiful Herbert stayed
huddled.

"Call her, David. She always comes when you call
her."

No word from David. Finally Lance retrieved Herbert and put her on David's lap. He kissed her and
drooled on her, but for all our efforts, Herbert did not
trigger one word.

The next night I asked, "David, do you know what
you'd like to do most?" He nodded.

"Spell it out." He had a wooden lapboard with the
letters of the alphabet pasted on. With his left hand
he spelled "go home."

"David, listen carefully. When you say 'home,' I'll
take you. It's very easy. You can laugh, so open your
mouth, take a deep breath, and say 'home.' Go ahead.
David, no one can do it for you. You have to say the
first word, then others will follow. Right now—say
'home.' "

He opened his mouth and faintly whispered, "home."

I was ecstatic! My prayers had been answered. He
had just said his first word, one week short of six
months after the accident. Generally speaking, if a
part of the motor-control system returns within a
six-month period, it indicates there will be no permanent damage. Running down the hall, I cried, "David's
talking."

The next visit, I said, "Hi, David."

He nodded.

"No more nodding. If you can say 'home,' you can
say 'hi.' Open your mouth, take a deep breath, and
say 'hi.' Do it right now."

"Hi." It was a faint whisper, but it was definitely a
"hi."

After he could say three words, nurse Betty told the
internist.

"David," he said, "I understand you're talking now.
Say 'home' for me."

No response.

"Come on, Dave," Betty persuaded. "You can, I heard you."

No response.

"Let me get Bob, his favorite orderly. He heard him too."

No response for Bob.

"Okay, David," said the internist. "Just remember, I give the orders around here and you're not going home until I hear it from you."

"Home."

"Very good, David." Turning to Betty, he continued, "See that he goes back to speech class tomorrow."

New Year's Day, while we were having dessert in the dining room with David, he spelled out on his lapboard, "I am just coming around."

"Do you mean you're becoming aware of what happened to you and where you are?"

He nodded. In the beginning, to promote recall, we had shown him a picture of his father's VW that he had totalled. He really gave no visible response. Now I raced back to his room and got the photo. Holding it in front of him, I asked, "Does this help to clarify things in your mind?"

He nodded and with his left hand spelled out, "I feel dumb."

"Don't, David. It's all water over the dam. The important thing is that you're here and getting better."

"Want to play chess?" his father asked.

He nodded. Chess is a thinking game—far beyond me—and his recollection was surprising. I must tell you his next word was "Mom." It never sounded so great. I attended all the speech meetings at Kessler, which were held every other week. David's therapist, Ruth Udell, was fabulous. In the beginning she placed coins on the table. "David, point to the dime, the penny, the nickel. Very good. Where is the door? Right." Elementary but necessary questions for one who has aphasia. Flashing pictures and words on the speech-machine screen, Ruth said, "David, match the proper word with the picture." She expected and she received. Now David began spelling out questions to her: "Where am I? What happened to me?" The answers were typed and pasted on his lapboard for him to read.

"I am at Kessler Institute in West Orange, New Jersey. I was in a car accident in July 1972, and am here for therapy. I will go home when I am better."

Red letter day—January 13. David came home for the day, six months after his accident. Darryl rode with him in our local ambulance. They arrived at 10:30 A.M. Three rescue workers transferred him onto the sofa bed in our TV room. Compared to his hospital bed he looked rather uncomfortable, but was perfectly content to lie there the whole day with Herbert and let us wait on him hand and foot. It was a very quiet day. The doctor did not want David exposed to confusion or a group of friends, and his word was law. At 7 P.M. the ambulance returned him to Kessler. It was a good day—a day I knew would come, a day I thanked God for, but also a day on which David did not utter one word.

Two weeks later he was allowed to come home overnight. John and I took our instructions for gluing on the sheath and position turning. He was turned every two hours throughout the night. This was a must to prevent bedsores, and we were grateful David didn't have any, nor did we want to take any chances. He also wore a cumbersome right leg and foot half-cast that was anchored with a never-ending Ace bandage. This was to straighten his slightly turned foot.

He arrived Saturday morning by our local ambulance. By noon David had his first visitor.

"David, good to see you home. Know who I am?"

We could tell he was trying to remember and no way would he give up. "Let me open my ski jacket." As soon as David saw the clerical collar he smiled and nodded. Father Ashe sat down.

"Can you remember when you first learned to ski? It wasn't easy. You kept falling, right? But you got up and tried again and again. What you're going through now isn't easy either, but you keep trying even when the going gets rough. I know you'll make it."

During the night, John and I set the alarm for every two hours. Turning looked so easy when we watched others, but for us it was an ordeal. Every pillow in the house was tucked somewhere around David, who slept through it all. Sunday night when we returned to Kessler, the nurse asked, "How did it go?"

"Fine."

"You're exhausted, right?"

"Right, but it's an exhaustion I've looked forward to."

After the third ambulance trip home, David had improved enough to come by car. It looked like moving day with wheelchair, lapboard (we used it for meals and games), stereo, headphones, clothes, medical supplies, and the lamb's wool fuzzy he slept on. All the way home we'd do therapy.

"David, watch the light and tell me when to go."

When it turned green, he said, "Go."

"Where is our street?"

He pointed left as we came to it.

"Which is our house?"

"Here."

By February 14, 1973, David was speaking short sentences. During our Friday night trips home, sometimes I had to pull the car to the side of the road in order to understand what he said. His tone was weak and breath control short. If after the second repeat I still didn't get it, I'd say, "Spell it out." He did, proving more progress. Physical parts of his body that had been classified zero were now poor and poor plus. At this point a molded plastic half-cast was put on his right arm every night. This was the arm that was originally locked to his chin. We would extend the arm as far as possible and then place it in the cast. It was anchored with an Ace bandage. The arm was coming down, but slowly. Trunk control had improved and new orders were issued—to the shower room in a chair.

Along with the good news, there was bad. David had gained twenty-seven pounds in two months, an unbelievable amount. More new orders: Move David to the diet table. During our monthly interview, Dr. Sullivan pointed out that David's residual damage was coordination, which would require years to overcome. The thought did not especially upset me. Coping with one day at a time had become my life style. As I was leaving, he said, "I meant to tell you, David saw our psychologist for the first time this month."

"Oh, really. How did he react?"

"Like a typical teen-ager. He said, 'Hi, shrink,' and the psychologist answered, 'Hi, kid.' "

It was one of those raw, windy March days good for Lipton's tea and heavy reading, but I was doing uninspiring housework when the phone rang. Relieved, I ran to answer. It was my friend Dorothea. We had met through the Newcomers' Club when we first moved to the area. As soon as she had heard of David's accident, she had come. Now she was asking, "Will you accept an electric hospital bed from the Woman's Club for David?"

My voice quivered. "I don't know what to say. I'm touched that people still want to do so much."

"We had a board meeting this morning and the vote was unanimous. Think it over."

"I'll check with the doctor at Kessler."

The doctor's advice: Take it.

John and Darryl set it up in the TV room. To say the room was overcrowded was the understatement of the year. Decor was out. David's needs were in. The first night we learned how much easier it was to position-turn him. At moments like this, I paused to reflect what a thing friendship is—a glimpse of God.

*   *   *

The following day my phone jingled at 8 A.M. Early morning or late evening calls make me antsy. I answered quickly.

"Mrs. Landvater, I'm calling from Kessler."

Fear washed over me.

"Before you read *The New York Times,* I want to tell you there was a fire in David's room last night, but don't worry, he's fine."

"Was anyone hurt?"

"No, but all David's personal belongings are gone. When you come in tonight bring clothes and shoes."

I hung up, numb, and yet my mind was functioning. Everything ruined. What rotten luck! David's stereo was in the repair shop and I had borrowed one. How do you tell a friend, her stereo burned last night. The scrapbook destroyed, too. It had so many cards for recall, and darn it, my new tape recorder. Suddenly the impact hit: God is good.

We learned the details that night. John, the patient in the bed next to David, was awakened by crackling, tooth-like orange flames shooting from David's closet across his head toward the curtain between them. John called out, but his voice was weak. Another roommate awakened.

"Fire! Get us out of here, you sons of bitches."

He got action. The night guard became Hercules, pulling David's bed out with the foot stoppers down, then returning for John as the flaming curtain fell. The bed nearest the door was taken out last. The fourth bed was empty and burned. *The New York Times* reported on March 5, 1973, "Thirty-nine patients, of which ten percent were ambulatory, were evacuated with efficiency and speed to the physical therapy room."

David's account: "It was scary." He waved his left hand over his head, showing how he kept the flames from sparking his hair. Bad as his short-term memory was, he remembered the fire and that he had been given oxygen. Even after the room was renovated, David never returned to 168.

Red letter day—March 20. David got black surgical high-top shoes. The right one had a short brace below the knee. Even though they were a far cry from the fad sandals, he was proud of them because standing balance had begun. No more tilt table. He had been on it twice a day since last September. Mentally, to quote the doctor, he continues to awaken. He and I were now doing simple crossword puzzles. David's high school counselor had been in touch and sent a school magazine, *Scope,* which had puzzles and other mind stimulation. We had found a paperback on writing your own story by filling in adjectives, adverbs, nouns, numbers, colors, and other parts of speech. It was exciting to hear what David had retained from English, but we had to practice patience. He had a delay in the thinking process; therefore it took time for his answers. Then too, unless he was forced to think, he didn't. For example, "David, what did you do today?"

"Nothing."

"Now think, get those brain cells working. Tell me one thing you did today."

"Eat."

"I'll buy that. What did you eat?"

"You only asked for one thing."

"Okay, smart aleck, tomorrow I'll ask for two things and add one each day."

And then it was May 6, David's eighteenth birthday. Over and over he'd ask, "How old am I?"

"Eighteen."

"But I don't remember being seventeen."

"Think. Your friends gave Eddie and you a party at Vickie's house. Didn't you pop the balloons in the foyer when you walked in?"

"Oh, yeah."

We decided to help stamp both birthdays in his memory bank by inviting the same friends. Kim spread the word. Barb baked the cake. Many came with presents to promote recall. Debbie brought his favorite dessert—eclairs. David was really happy. He knew everyone by name and initiated some talk. But the very next day he asked, "How old am I?"

The month of June brought exciting things. For one, it was our twenty-fifth wedding anniversary. The doctor gave permission for David to go out for dinner. He looked terrific dressed in tie and jacket. When the waitress asked, "Will anyone be having a cocktail?" David answered quickly and clearly, "I'll have a whiskey sour."

"David, when did you ever have a whiskey sour?"

"Mother!" yelled our other sons.

Before his accident he had a habit of ordering the most expensive thing on the menu. True to form, he had lobster. Again and again he proved there was nothing wrong with his long-term memory, but the short-term remained a serious problem. I kept hanging onto the theory that the short-term memory is the last thing to return. The next day David remembered he had one whiskey sour. As the doctor said, "Things you'd expect him to remember, he doesn't. And the things you'd never think he'd remember, he does."

June brought another special day, one of pride and happiness as our third son, Lance, graduated from Franklin and Marshall College in Pennsylvania. Although I did not attend the exercises, Darryl, Barb, Grandpa, and his father did. Lance was now ready to face medical school, and since David's accident he was more determined than ever.

After seven months at Kessler, bladder training was started. David could ease up on his intake of cranberry juice. We had learned why everyone drank it: Cranberry juice is a diuretic; it flushes the plumbing system and helps prevent bladder infections. At home I bought it by the gallon and David was sick of it.

Night-position turning was dismissed. Thanks and

credit go to all those who faithfully turned David throughout the nights. How do I know for sure that it was done? Not one bedsore is proof. And for us, no more setting the alarm every two hours over weekends. During this monthly interview the doctor announced, "David is moving out of the beginning stages of recovery."

His words hit me like a bee sting. It had now been ten and a half months since his accident. I thought he'd been out for some time. However, there was no question in my mind that Kessler knew what they were doing, and I accepted their word.

The Woman's Club's generosity in giving the hospital bed had promoted interest from civic organizations, churches, schools, and individuals. On June 11, they sponsored a bridge benefit for the David Landvater Fund. My friend asked for a picture, and David consented. John took and developed it. At first David was critical, photography being his thing, but when he got front-page coverage in several newspapers he said, "Not bad." It was a beautiful day for me. Approximately two hundred friends came, and the donations exceeded the cost of the bed. We decided to use the extra money to enlarge our half bath and the bedroom doorway on the first floor. Still the fund remained open.

Weight lifting, along with constant therapy, had overdeveloped David's left side, especially his left hand. He loved to shake hands. Shake is a loose word. He squeezed until the victim cried out in pain and self-defense. The day he flattened my ring band and imprinted its design on my finger I yelled, "Never again!" However, the family and visitors thought it great sport to let David show off his strength. Even the internist agreed until . . .

"Dave," said Betty, "did you tell your mother what you did to our internist today?"

"What did I do?"

"Don't tell me you forgot! How convenient. You crushed his hand so hard he fell to his knees."

Using the tone that meant, "You've got to be kidding," David said, "I didn't break it."

"Lucky for you." Turning to me Betty admitted, "They honestly thought it was broken, but the X-ray was negative. Everyone has been informed—no one, I mean *no one,* is to pick up David's left hand."

"Good," I nodded. "Maybe now everyone will make him use his right hand. That gives me an idea. David, let's see if you can turn the knob of the Etch-a-Sketch using your right hand. You know that's how you got your left hand working."

David's right arm was now down to about an 80-degree angle, and he could move his fingers. It took a tremendous amount of effort and time, but he could do it. The problem was that it was easier to use his left hand. Extending his thumb and first finger, he zeroed in on the knob, but turning it was another matter. He just didn't have the strength or coordination. Whenever he was trying to master a new movement, I busied myself. Watching only added more tension to the already heavy atmosphere. In time he got one short weak line.

Hugging him, I exclaimed, "That's fantastic! Keep trying every night and soon you'll be making lots of lines."

Periodically Kessler had entertainment for their patients, and every Monday night was bingo. Bingo was not David's idea of a fun evening, nor would he go into the gym for other programs. Once I insisted and it was a disaster. Although he was not subject to fits of laughter, he and another patient got the giggles. If David didn't want to do something, he found a way not to.

Every Friday when I arrived to bring him home for the weekend a volunteer was playing the piano for the patients. Bob, an orderly, would sing along when time permitted. He had a good tenor voice.

"David," I asked, "do you think Bob would mind if I joined him in a song?"

He almost shouted, "Don't do it, Dot." (Sometimes he'd call me by my first name just to bug me.)

The patients thought it was a grand idea. Bob and I sang "On the Street Where You Live." David thought it was so terrible he wheeled his chair down the hall, but the patients asked if we couldn't sing on a week night when everyone was there. That was all the encouragement we needed. I arranged for a friend of mine, a professional pianist, to accompany us. Bob and I sang completely unrehearsed and in between our numbers the patients called out requests. Phil was extremely talented and could play everything. It was a fun evening. David sat through it all with that look, "Not bad, but I'd never tell them." With or without his approval, we did repeat programs.

For the July celebration, Kessler had a young banjo player. For the first time David yelled, "More." We were very happy to see spontaneous responses. Later in the afternoon, I found three patients and lots of assistants to play Monopoly. It was my newest mind-stimulating idea. An hour later everyone was ready to quit except David, who was winning. His recall was thrilling to watch, along with his old nerve for gambling.

August brought new problems. The Physical Therapy Department wanted to instruct me for home exercises. That put some doubt and fear in my mind. I knew Kessler couldn't keep David forever, but surely they weren't ready to discharge him? When I arrived, David's roommate was in the lobby.

"David's going home in two weeks," he announced. "They told him this morning."

I froze, wax white. The receptionist and I had a collision of blind stares. "It's true," she said with a compassionate voice. "What will you ever do?"

"I don't know," I mumbled.

The physical therapist called me. She demonstrated sitting balance, leg exercises, and right-arm stretching. (Three different casts had been used to get David's arm to an 80-degree angle. Now only time and constant stretching could hopefully extend it to a normal position.) All exercises were to be done daily, twice if possible. She then told me the internist wanted to see me.

I returned to the lobby. My fear grew with each passing minute. The certainty of what was going to happen and the uncertainty as to what I would do took over. I knew Kessler's policy—they keep the patient as long as they progress. David continued to progress slowly, but it was progress. Why then were they sending him home? Exhaustion drained me. My body was tired and my mind was tired. I felt I had no weapon with which to fight. "What do you think, God?"

I walked into the internist's office. I sat. He stood.

"Mrs. Landvater, this morning I decided to discharge David in two weeks, but I have changed my mind."

Relief flooded over me. *Thank You, God.*

"As long as David continues to improve, Kessler will keep him. You're an intelligent woman and I'm sure you realize David has many serious problems. I hope we just don't bring him to the brink and that's as far as he can go. That is a possibility."

I left his office with a new opinion of the internist. He was doctor enough and man enough to have changed his decision, but my heart was heavy. To be realistic about David's future was overwhelming.

Seven days later our son Greg was hospitalized. For the first time since David's accident it was hard to be positive and enthusiastic. I felt as if I were carrying a five-hundred-pound burden around, but when Dr. Sullivan said, "Let us worry about David. Don't you be concerned," my old philosophy, nothing is insurmountable, came through.

By the end of August, David took his first steps at the walking bars. They were not easy, normal steps as you and I take, but they were a beginning. Standing balance would have to be perfected first. He had progressed to eating independently, using his left hand,

and it was no longer necessary to have a nurse stand by in the event he choked. David was learning to handle his own difficulties.

Time passed. It was September.

"David," I said, "Father Ashe called today. He said to tell you he's leaving Berkeley Heights but his prayers will continue for you."

"I remember what he told me."

"What?" Hoping against hope, I waited with bated breath.

"He said, 'David, this is the greatest challenge you will ever have to face, but I know you can do it.' "

"That's remarkable! Father told you that while you were very under at Overlook, giving the PT therapist a rough time."

"I know," he answered.

Red letter day—September 11. David's brother Darryl, who has a pilot's license, took him flying. Acting out my role of mother, I was very apprehensive, but when Dr. Sullivan gave permission I could only worry. To this day I consider it a miracle that they physically got David inside the small plane. Anyway, David loved it and it was a tremendous morale booster.

With the passing of time, more and more people became involved with David. Several members of the Presbyterian Youth Fellowship in our town began to drop in for about an hour, early on Saturday nights. David accepted them, but since he hadn't known them before his accident, he was rather lukewarm. On the other hand, he loved to play Monopoly, and they were accommodating. The beauty of this story is that the young people didn't give up, especially Ward. Ward had found the answer to handling David: "I treat him just like any other guy." Soon David was teaching Ward chess.

*   *   *

On certain days some feel they'd like to rip their phone from the wall. For the past fourteen months it seemed the voices on the other end of my phone were filled with love, compassion, and willingness to help. Today it was the young chaplain who had been at Overlook Hospital when David was admitted. Over and over I was grateful for those who really became involved. Ofter our friends would wait until after visiting hours at Kessler to have dinner with us. No one ever suggested our leaving early. They all knew I was obsessed with stimulating David. No way would I let him just sit even for a short time.

David continued to become more "with it." In speech he printed, "Man, oh man, I had one hell of an accident." Now he was turning out handmade items like a machine in occupational therapy. You name it, he had made it. And David decided to play bingo. Actually, one night Greg inspired him by saying, "Let's see what we can win." Winning was easy, as the callers allowed three winners before clearing the card, and David loved to win. He gave his prizes to the therapists and nurses he especially liked. From then on he played every Monday night.

As November approached we realized David's days were numbered at Kessler. We had been there long enough to see the turnover. The average patient's stay was three to four months. This month would mark a full year for David. Besides, his attitude was changing.

"I hate this place," he griped.

"But David, they've done so much for you. You were considered comatose when you arrived, and look at you now."

"Oh, yeah. Well, you don't know what I have to put up with."

Using a firm motherly tone, I snapped, "Knock it off! They all love you around here. You've become a Kessler fixture."

Silently Dr. Sullivan's words rushed forward: "When David becomes more unhappy, I'll be more happy."

It was decided between the doctors, therapists, and psychologist that David needed a new challenge. The time had come to call a tutor. We were delighted. From the time I knew David could hear in ICU, I had pushed and pulled for recall, always testing his ability to think, understand, and reason, because of the neurologist's words, "We have reason to believe he will be a vegetable." I didn't believe them, but the thought had been planted. Now the truth would be known. Kessler's psychologist contacted David's school system and a tutor arrived November 21, 1973. Testing began. The tutor came three times a week in the late afternoon for about an hour. David responded well, although he tired easily due to his double vision, laborious printing with his left hand, and his slow thinking process. The sweat that ran down his face proved he was putting out and not about to give up.

November also brought football games.

"David," I asked, "how would you like to go to a football game at your school?"

"I'd like that."

His friends responded and the social contact with his peers was another ego booster. On Thanksgiving Day there was some kind of mix-up. In the end, his father and I took him to the game. All the way he complained, "I find this very degrading to have my parents take me to the game." The word degrading pleased me no end—proof again that his vocabulary was not so terribly limited as predicted.

"Don't worry, David. Your father and I will disappear the minute we deliver you."

There are certain advantages to carrying a wheelchair. We drove right up to the gate. There stood our family doctor.

"David," he smiled, "let me do the honor of wheeling you down to the front row."

John and I became lost in the crowd; however, not

so lost that we missed the enjoyment of seeing David relate to his peers.

It was again the Christmas month, time for another conference with Dr. Sullivan. He and I calmly sat facing each other across his wide desk, each realistically knowing what was coming. He spoke first.

"David is ready to go home." His tone was warm.

I nodded. "After being in hospitals for seventeen and a half months, I'd be ready too."

"When would you like to take him?"

"How about next Friday?"

"Fine. Outpatient therapy days at Kessler are Monday through Friday. I suggest three days for David. How does that sound to you?"

"Good. We'll take Monday, Wednesday, and Friday. I would prefer mornings if that's possible."

"I think it can be arranged. I'll schedule him for one half-hour of speech and one hour of physical therapy." He made several notations on paper, then looked up. "I'd like him to continue with our psychologist once a month."

"All right." It seemed like a good idea to me. He put down his pen and looked me square in the eyes. "We like to follow up with monthly physicals for our outpatients. An appointment will be set up and you'll be notified of the time. I guess that's about it, unless you have something on your mind." He sat back in his chair and wanted.

"No," I kind of caressed the word. I knew Kessler had been more than fair in keeping David for thirteen and a half months, and I was fully aware and most appreciative of the miraculous things they had done for him. Another chapter in David's rehabilitation was closed, but a new one was opening. I gave no wails of "How am I going to cope" or "suppose I can't cope." We both knew I had a job to do and I'd learn how to do it.

He walked me to the door. We gave no goodbyes,

no thank-you's; it was not the end. In the very beginning I thought, "What is one year out of David's
young life?" Now I was thinking, "What are three
years out of David's life?" I flashed back to the night
of the accident.

"God," I had asked, "you wouldn't take my seventeen-year-old boy, would you?"

Time.

PART THREE

Home

Friday, December 14, 1973, 5 P.M.—Kessler's automatic door swung out. David was leaving. Just like my strong conviction that one day he would wake up, I dogmatically had believed he would walk out of Kessler. He did not. I pushed him in his new five-hundred-dollar wheelchair. He had been gone seventeen months—thirteen and a half at Kessler and three and a half at Overlook Hospital. We were both delighted to be going home.

What was his condition? I think the Social Service Director phrased it best. "You understand we aren't finished with David. We believe he will go further, but right now he has had all the institutional life he can take."

Medically, he was initiating spontaneous speech and speaking more clearly, but by no means fluently. Balance had improved; however, he could not stand alone. Even a sitting position was wobbly. He assisted in personal hygiene, dressing, transferring to and wheeling his chair. Using his left hand he fed himself, but could not hold a mug independently. In short, he required twenty-four-hour-a-day attention.

Realizing our split-level house wasn't conducive to a wheelchair, we had enlarged the half bath. For the second time our plumber was all heart.

"I found this corner washbowl in stock," he proudly announced. "Your only charge will be the labor." Compassion alone is beautiful, but when it replaces the dollar, it's more beautiful.

David had access to the hall, TV room, bedroom, and half bath. My legs began the never-ending run up and down the stairs. Two days later my orthopedic sandals walked out of retirement.

December 17, 7:30 A.M.—David began his first day as an outpatient.

"Don't mess," he'd insist during dressing. He even had a button hooker. Pushing the hook through the buttonhole, he caught the button and pulled it closed. I started the top one and he finished. I was allowed to put on his socks, surgical high-top shoes, and tuck in his shirttail. It was a painful experience to observe David dress. All the ordinary tasks you and I take for granted were tedious, frustrating, and time-consuming. Quickly I learned to walk away, busying myself with routine chores, and at the same time to keep a watchful eye open. Besides, it gave David a feeling of independence.

8:15 A.M.—breakfast.

Kessler had given David a metal clamp-on plate guard to prevent spilling. It worked great. Holding the spoon with his left hand, he carefully guided the food into his mouth. On days he had my famous Czechoslovakian pancakes, I would place a piece in his right hand. Moving his hand to his mouth was no easy task, but not impossible. Often the food would drop. If after the second try he didn't succeed, he'd cheat a little by bending his head to meet his hand. My theory was "Use your right hand—that's how you got your left hand working." David agreed.

8:45 A.M.—brush teeth.

"Easy does it, David. You're making your gums bleed."

The ataxia caused the brush to go wild, but with repetition he'd master control. In the meantime I prayed, "Please God, don't let him ruin his gums." At my age I thought about things like gums.

8:55 A.M. —transfer into car.

"Slowly, David, let's not have both of us roll down the driveway."

Some days he'd smile, "Pretty good, huh?" Others, he'd drop his voice to show disgust, admitting, "Pretty lousy, huh?" Either way we joked. David had a marvelous attitude. He knew he had to slow down in order to control beginning movements or he'd lose his balance. I raced the wheelchair around the car, folded it and rolled it onto a board behind the seat. I had learned this trick from seeing a movie at Kessler. I remember the day I got the board from our local lumber mill. When the salesman asked, "May I help you?" his voice alone dampened my spirits.

"Yes," I answered. "I have a fun project for you. At least I hope you'll see it that way. I carry a wheelchair and need a board to fit over the well in the back of the driver's seat.

He hastened to answer, "We don't have anything like that." I could feel his sigh of relief.

"Oh, listen, any old scrap board will do." My words tumbled on top of each other as I told about the movie.

"What are the exact dimensions of this board you want?"

"Gee, I don't know. Why don't you come outside and take a look at my car?" We exchanged silent glances. I didn't move a muscle. His face tightened.

"All right. Lead me to your car."

Within minutes he found a scrap board, cut it, and placed it over the well. He was almost happy. "I think this will do."

"If not," I reasoned, "I'll bring the wheelchair back."

"No, no," he blurted. "Don't bring your troubles

back to me. Anyway, there's no charge." If he hadn't been such a grump, I'd have shown him the board was working out fine.

9 A.M.—off to Kessler.

David would have one half-hour of speech therapy, followed by one hour of physical therapy. I usually fell into a gas line (this was during the gas shortage) or chatted with others who transported patients. I had become a Kessler fixture myself and by this time had learned what to do while waiting: sit down and relax.

12 noon—lunch.

1 P.M.—mental stimulation.

During this time David did anagrams, crossword puzzles, multiplication problems, various games from the *Grab a Pencil* paperback book, as well as all kinds of small physical and brain-buster games. The object was for David to put out more than the day before, but not for me to push him over the line of total frustration. It was tricky to achieve the balance, especially if we were both tired.

2 P.M.—exercises.

David sat on the edge of his hospital bed with feet flat on the floor to strengthen trunk control. At the same time he'd repeat after me words or sentences for speech homework. In a lying position he'd move each leg—up, down, and out. Push-ups were next. Although his right arm was moving and bending, it was very difficult for him to get it straight up and move it back. He'd touch the headboard in back of him, then open his fingers and pull out a Kleenex we had tucked into his shirt pocket. It took a lot of patience, but he could do it. I doubt that I'll ever pass as a heel-cord therapist, but I was faithful in trying.

3 P.M.—nap.

David needed to be what I called bright-eyed and bushy-tailed for his tutors.

3:30 to 5 P.M.—tutors.

Kessler's psychologists had requested two tutors through David's public school system before he was discharged. The tutor who had gone to Kessler now came to our home on Monday, Wednesday, and Friday. A new math tutor came Tuesday and Thursday. I had read many books on the brain, and actual brain-damage cases similar to David's and, surprising as it may seem, math was usually the first subject to return. I was most anxious to see his response.

5 to 6 P.M.—TV.

David loved to watch "The Flintstones." Remember, he started that at Overlook Hospital. In spite of his double vision, he seemed able to see the show and follow the plot.

6 P.M.—dinner.

Unfortunately, there was nothing wrong with David's appetite. He loved to eat and I loved to cook, but we both had to control our impulses. He had grown in all directions within the last year, and extra weight would only add another handicap.

7 P.M.—homework; repeat exercises.

8 P.M.—bed bath.

We had purchased a shower chair, stool, and hand shower control, but it was not feasible at this time to get David up the two short flights of stairs to the family bathroom. I handed him the soaped washcloth and he took over.

"Come on, put it in your right hand," I'd scold. Of course it was easier and faster to use his left hand, but he responded to my prodding and pushing. He was beautiful.

8:30 P.M.—lights out.

David's schedule was regimented and predictable. My family chided me for being too pushy and strict, but I saw no other way. Rehabilitation is a concentrated and repetitious program. I had learned that at Kessler.

9 P.M.—chores.

I cleaned up the kitchen, took a shower, and literally fell into bed. One week of this routine and every muscle ached. Our weight should have been reversed—

mine is one hundred and fifteen pounds and David's one hundred and fifty pounds.

Christmas was coming all too quickly. It arrived the second week after David's discharge from Kessler. Although my family from Pennsylvania couldn't come because of the gas shortage, Grandpa came. David had made all his gifts with his left hand in occupational therapy with the help of Sandy. She had a tremendous rapport with David. Proudly he passed out his wrapped surprises: for Grandpa, a doormat with his initial in the middle; for Darryl and Barb, a marbleized ceramic chess set; for Greg, wooden bookends with a hammered copper ship; for Lance, a gold leather woven belt; for Father, a leather key case; for me, a multicolored ceramic vase and a wooden recipe holder. Over and over he'd ask, "Do you really like it?"

"We sure do," we kept repeating again and again.

He beamed, "I made it all by myself." It was a very special Christmas. Our family was whole again.

For weeks David had been planning a New Year's Eve party. Every night he printed a few invitations with his left hand while at Kessler. They read, "OPEN HOUSE—7 P.M."

"David, put R.S.V.P. at the bottom."

"No."

"I have to know how many will come."

"They'll all come. They'll crash it."

"Kids don't crash parties any more."

"You'll see," he threatened.

"Okay, if they do, Greg will be the bouncer."

Greg and I had everything ready, with David's approval. Beer, a punch bowl of whiskey sours (weak according to John, strong according to me), onion dip with chips, hot dogs in biscuit blankets, and our famous pretzels from Pennsylvania. Greg found two of David's homemade bottle candles in his room and added them to the buffet table. Forty classmates came. David was right—we hadn't invited half of them, but no one got bounced. David was remarkable! He thrilled us by knowing everyone by name, once again giving definite proof that there was nothing wrong with his long-term memory. When one of his friends said, "Dave, I don't know if I should have beer or a whiskey sour," he quickly answered, "Beer and liquor, never felt sicker. Liquor and beer, never fear." Everyone laughed. It was one of those peer jokes David remembered. At the final countdown he was sitting on the hospital bed with a girl on each side lending support. One minute after midnight David nodded out.

After the holidays we settled into a normal routine. Monday, Wednesday, and Friday mornings were spent at Kessler. Tuesday and Thursday mornings we went to the local county hospital, which was only five minutes from our house. Our family doctor had made the arrangements and Kessler's therapy was continued. This meant David would have physical therapy five days a week.

The day I hand-delivered the reports to the county hospital is still vivid in my mind. I felt stuck to the car seat, holding a bulging unsealed manila envelope. Inside were David's medical history from Overlook Hospital and his monthly rehab reports from Kessler. I read them. I understood more of the medical jargon than I thought I would. I turned off the car motor and never even felt the cold January air creep in. The reports confirmed that David's being alive was a miracle, and that doctor's predictions can be wrong. The overall reports from Overlook were gloomy and pessimistic. However, the final one said, "Patient responds to verbal stimuli." The reports from Kessler showed slow but constant progress. The first one was the most surprising. It said, "Patient is often found in fetal position while sleeping." What did I think about his future after reading them?

Time.

*   *   *

January brought new problems. When David had been admitted to Kessler he had never felt the impact of adjusting because he was in a comatose state. I recall that many patients in his room found the first couple weeks tense and frustrating. They griped and complained constantly. The orderlies and nurses just shrugged their shoulders, "It always takes a little time to adjust to us, but we're patient." Now that David was more alert and aware of what was going on around him, he felt the pangs of adjustment at the county hospital. I was told that he didn't look where he was going. He ran his chair into other patients. He would rather look at the therapist's legs than do the project; and this final sin, he told the PT therapist, "You don't know what you're doing."

"David," I cried, "they think you're a sex maniac."

He smiled. "She had nice legs."

"Well, you made her nervous. So tomorrow, forget her legs. And another thing, don't tell the people in PT they don't know what they're doing."

"They treat me like a baby."

"If you want to be treated like an eighteen-year-old, then act like one." I appealed to our family doctor and the doctor of rehab at the county hospital. Both explained, "Dave, hang in there. We're trying to help you."

Both recognized he wanted to walk more than anything else in the world. I watched through the glass window door in PT. David was stooped; he lunged forward at the parallel bars. His left hand gripped the metal like a vise. Even though the window I could see his knuckles were white. A therapist supported his right side. He picked up his left leg and socked it down. It jutted off to the side, throwing his balance farther off. The right leg eventually dragged halfway along. His legs and feet would not do what he wanted them to do. Big beads of sweat rolled down his face and soaked through his shirt. He tried again and again until his right leg became spastic, trembling and shaking. I felt sick. Fear began to creep in. The doctor at Kessler had said before his discharge, "We don't know

if we can ever get David out of his wheelchair."
Swallowing a lump and blinking back hot tears, I
opened the door, and then, forcing myself to be cheerful, I rather weakly called, "David, you're walking!"

"Yeah." He sounded discouraged.

"It'll get easier. You know everything has been as
slow as molasses in January, but it's all coming back."

Twice a week we sandwiched an eye appointment
into our day. David had an ulcerated cornea in the
right eye. This was the third time his left hand had
accidentally poked and scratched the cornea. These
mishaps were caused by the ataxia in his left hand.
Normally the cornea heals itself within twenty-four
hours when closed and pressure bandaged. For David
it took weeks because his whole right side was less
responsive.

It seemed to me all thirty-one days of January in
1974 were cold and messy, a combination of sleet,
snow, and slush. The eye doctor's office was on the
main thoroughfare, with no parking lot. Time and
again my friend Luella would meet us in front of the
building. She'd dash to the corner, asking if we could
illegally park. If the man in blue wasn't there, she'd
sit in my car while David and I hurried to the fifth
floor. Dr. Romas was our family eye physician, and
had seen David at Overlook Hospital.

"When I awoke this morning and saw more snow,"
he said, "I thought of calling you to postpone the
appointment until tomorrow."

"I thought of it too, but the patch is coming loose."

He examined the eye. "There's no change." His
tone was flat.

"What does that mean after five weeks?"

"I think the time has come to suture the eyelid shut.
Opening the bandage every third day is disturbing the
healing process. After it's closed he won't have to wear
a patch and this will give his skin a chance to heal
from the tape." He pulled a medical book off the shelf

and opened it to a diagram. "This is how I'll close the lid."

"I guess we don't have any alternative, do we?"

"Not really. We'll admit him as an outpatient at Orange Memorial Hospital on Wednesday. I'll make the necessary arrangements. Do you know where it is?"

"No, but I'll find it." David appeared nonplussed. I think he had so much pain from the eye that he welcomed anything. Luella was waiting in my car, and when I told her the latest verdict she suggested, "Why don't we take David out for lunch?"

"Do you know a place where we can get the wheelchair in?"

"Sure."

"Lead the way."

The restaurant was on a corner and the parking lot farther down the street, so I pulled into a snowplowed dry-cleaning lot. Together we wheeled David along a narrow, shoveled path on the sidewalk. It was a tight squeeze. Two men walking toward us stopped.

"Girls," they volunteered, "you should use the road. It'd be easier pushing."

When they passed I groaned, "Isn't that just like a man. They're great for telling you what to do but don't help you do it." Luella agreed.

By the time we reached the restaurant door we were both huffing and puffing like steam engines. Luella opened the door and two narrow steps faced us.

"How are we gonna get him up?" I wasn't about to give up, but my brow creased into a healthy frown.

"I'll find someone to help." Luella returned in minutes with two men from the bar. They looked like furniture movers. Gingerly they lifted David and chair up the steps. No problem.

When the waitress asked, "May I take your order?" David answered with great charm, "I'll have a beer." She was pretty, young, and exceptionally nice to David. He in turn was enamored with her. Needless to say, he enjoyed his lunch and managed very well minus his usual eating aids. The waitress gave him lots of napkins. The same two men at the bar jumped up and took David down the steps as we left. Looking up at them David said, "Thank you."

"That's okay," they answered, "glad to do it."

"I'd like you to know," I said, "what good Samaritans you've been today. David has been in a hospital for eighteen months and this is his first lunch out."

"Eighteen months!" Those two strapping men had tears in their eyes as they shook their heads, muttering, "Eighteen months!"

As soon as I awoke the next morning, I ran to the window. It was our day for the eye operation.

"I can't believe it, there must be three more inches of the white stuff out there. I'm beginning to hate snow."

"What time are you to be at the hospital?" John called from the shower.

"One P.M."

"By then it'll be melted."

I wasn't convinced. Furthermore, I had to drive to Kessler in it. On snowy, slippery days David transferred into my car inside the garage, then slid over to the passenger side. It was extremely hard for him to move his right side underneath the steering wheel, but far more safe.

The sun did shine and melted the snow on the main roads. David and I had lunch at a nearby restaurant before going to the hospital. Since David was being admitted as an outpatient and would only be having a local anesthesia, he was allowed to eat. After yesterday's success, I encouraged David to go out. My philosophy was that people will always stare at someone in a wheelchair, so get used to it.

We arrived at the emergency entrance promptly at 1 P.M. The man salting the area helped unload David. After being admitted he was taken to the OR room. I waited. For the first hour I was calm as a cucumber, knowing it wasn't a serious operation. Then my eyes began flitting from the big wall clock to the door, all the while telling myself it was nothing compared to what this boy had been through. Nevertheless, I was sure glad to see Dr. Romas finally walk through the door smiling.

"The operation was a success and David's in recovery now. I'll take you up."

Gee, I thought, I hadn't prepared him for the recovery room. As a matter of fact, the thought had never crossed my mind. As the doctor opened the door the nurse said, "He's been calling for you."

"Get me out of here," David cut in.

"David," I said, "stop yelling. You'll disturb the other patients."

We all began to help dress him. I cannot stress the compassion these people had for David. They knew he had reached the saturation point with hospitals.

"Is anyone with you?" asked our doctor.

"No."

"Where's your car?"

"Across the street in the lot."

"You get it and I'll wait with David so I can help you."

Perhaps he felt our exhaustion, for by this time it was 5 P.M.—David and I had left our house at 9 A.M. This doctor was quite a guy.

The first time we had the eye checked at the doctor's office after the surgery, David pointed to the bookcase. "Look at that clock."

"Oh, yeah. I never saw any like that before. It's all face." The face was glass and nothing surrounded it.

"You know how it works?"

"Sure, the hands turn."

"No, the face turns."

"I don't think so, David."

"I know so." The door opened and Dr. Romas walked in.

"Doctor," said David, "do you know how that clock works?"

"Yes, the hands turn."

"No, the face turns." Walking over to the clock, the doctor turned something in the back.

"See, the hands turn."

"No, the face turns. I know."

"David," I cut in, "we'll ask your father when we get home. Now let the doctor check your eye. He's a busy man."

"But I know the face turns." He was getting very up-tight about the fact that we didn't believe him.

"Okay!" My expression said to the doctor, "Sometimes he gets an idea and you can't change it." We were relieved to know the eye was doing fine. That evening David and I told his father about the clock.

"Dave's right. He and I saw a clock like that a long time ago."

"See, I knew," David exclaimed. "Didn't I tell you?"

"I apologize for doubting you and I'm thrilled you remembered."

Jumping up, I kissed the back of his head. I had acquired this habit at Kessler. Whenever I pushed him down the hall I couldn't seem to resist stooping over and kissing the back of his head. In the beginning he wasn't able to do anything about it. Later, when he could talk, he said, "Stop that, Dot." I smiled, mumbling something about how I couldn't fight the impulse, especially when his hair was squeaky clean. However, from then on I saved my kisses for shampoo days only, and David accepted them if I was quicker than he.

David tolerated the tutors and complained to me that they gave him baby work. When I spoke privately to the math tutor, she informed me that she was still testing. Through a friend, I got some sixth grade math from her school. David did it and I proudly presented it to his tutor. She agreed to give him something more challenging. But as the days passed, I became more and more unhappy with the situation. I talked with the director of specialized education through the school system.

"Mrs. Landvater," he said, "these are specialized teachers. You must be patient."

"But David can add twelve plus three. He knows the difference between a penny, a nickel, and a quarter. I know he's not ready to return to the senior class, but let's not go to extremes in the other direction. They're undoing all Kessler has done."

I hung up with a sick headache. We were worlds apart. However, the next day the other tutor (David had two) arrived with a new workbook: *Your Future, Your Job*. The lessons described a fireman, a postman, a policeman, and a photographer. After a long hassle David agreed to do the lesson "The Photographer" since that was his most recent hobby. I began reading the assignment and halfway through the first page David interrupted, "Wait a minute! Why are we doing this kid stuff?"

I was hard put to answer. "David, do it just to prove you can."

Determined to make an all-out effort, I appealed to the tutor again.

"Couldn't you stimulate David in English? He's writing poems for his speech therapist at Kessler. His latest is:

> My eyes are weary,
> My skin is torn,
> My soul is crushed
> But I'm alive,
> And that's just about
> Everything."

"Very good," he said. He seemed impressed. "I'll see what I can do." Another workbook arrived. The first homework assignment was to capitalize the proper nouns in a sentence.

"Are you kiddin' me?" David protested.

"Just do one to prove you can."

"I did that the last time. I want to go back to my school."

Right then and there an idea was born. A classmate of David's and I took him to visit his high school. We saw several of David's teachers and his counselor. I felt them out concerning the possibility of David sitting in on a class; they saw no problem but said it would have to be cleared through the principal.

Twice David and I returned but were unable to see the principal. The third time we got the vice-principal, who referred us to the school psychologist. She was young and pretty but not too enthused about David's returning to Governor Livingston High. Maybe she had been informed to some extent about David from the social worker. The week after his discharge from Kessler, the social worker from the school system came to our house. Her visit was disappointing.

"I see," she commented, "that you have three sons who have been to very good colleges—Cornell, Lehigh, and one in premed at Franklin and Marshall. Can you accept David at the sixth grade level?"

She struck a raw nerve. My eyes popped and my mouth opened wide. I knew I was shouting. "Only when it is proven to me. They haven't even finished testing him."

"Oh, I think they have. Perhaps you're unaware that we have special diplomas for cases like David's. How would you feel about accepting one?"

"No way. We're only beginning his mind rehabilitation. No one knows how far he can go."

As far as I was concerned she was dismissed, but I resisted the urge to throw her out.

Now the school psychologist was introducing David and me to a speech therapist, a remedial reading teacher, and the social worker. If I were to objectively describe David, I'd have to say his trunk posture was droopy as he sat in his wheelchair. He held his right hand fisted. It looked crippled. He wore a grotesque eye patch which covered most of the right side of his face, and his speech was thready. The remedial reading teacher spoke first.

"Mrs. Landvater, you can't be serious about having

David sit in on a German class. Why would you ever want him to take German?"

My bright smile evaporated. "Why don't you ask David?"

David spoke right up, "I had German two years and I like Mr. Haas."

"We just talked with him," I volunteered, "and he has no objection to David sitting in."

Another teacher gave me an unreal look. "Aren't you pushing too much? He looks tired."

"At Kessler he had five hours of therapy a day, plus the tutor."

"You understand, we have the fire laws to consider."

"I'll stand outside the door and be fully responsible, if you like." I felt like a computer spitting out answers.

"But we have the other students to consider. We don't know how they will accept David."

My computer went dead. There was a silent embarrassed pause. I'll never know how I managed to swallow my thoughts. The psychologist saved everyone by asking, "How are the tutors working out?"

"You tell her, David."

"No good. They give me baby work."

I don't even know what she answered. Frustration had killed my spirit. No way could I coerce these people to let David sit in on a class once a week for a month as a trial run. Further discussion was pointless. We left. As we headed home, David mumbled, "I can't believe it." His tone was filled with hurt. I couldn't believe it either. He had come so far. Why was the school system dragging their heels? I recalled what the speech therapist at Kessler had told me: "Your most frustrating experience will be when you get to the school system." Ruth was one hundred percent right and it was maddening.

The following day at Kessler, Dr. Sullivan met me in the hall.

"Come into my office," he demanded, looking very stern. I felt as if I were in a bucket of hot water. The question was, how did I get into it?

"Well," he said, "you certainly upset the whole high school yesterday with your visit. They called me. I realize you're a concerned mother, but David is not ready to return to the classroom. I thought you knew that."

His words hit me like a ton of bricks. I had been at Kessler a long time. Together we had been through many traumatic experiences, and I had nothing but the utmost respect for this doctor. But for all my courage, philosophy, faith, and hope, there were times when life was most difficult. This was one. And yet I knew I had a responsibility to David. Picking up the pieces of myself, I bored my eyes into his. "Do I get a chance to tell my side of the story?" I knew I was beet red and shouting.

"Go ahead."

"The psychologist had all these people there and David and I felt as though we were up on the public block while they fired questions right and left. It was awful."

Within five minutes he had evaluated the situation and was leading me to Kessler's psychologist.

"Mrs. Landvater is having some trouble with the school system," he said. "I want you to arrange a meeting between yourself and the school's psychologist. She's been through enough. Let's give her our support and help."

Expelling a centuries-old sigh, I smiled. With Kessler backing David and me, we could conquer the world.

A few days later David came down with a twenty-four-hour virus. He no sooner recovered from that when he developed a pain in his right side. At first our family doctor considered appendicitis because the area was highly sensitive. Two days later the pain localized itself in the kidney area. A specimen revealed bacteria. I knew stones are very prevalent in patients who are immobile. Could it be stones? I hoped not. However, I didn't want to take any chances; rushing right down to the A & P, I bought a gallon of cranberry juice. David had gotten sick of it as a daily part of his diet for over a year, and I was lax in pushing it. It was used at Kessler to help eliminate bladder infections and hopefully prevent flux or stones from forming. A week passed. He was not responding to the antibiotic. In fact, he was getting worse because of the continued low-grade temperature, which left him fatigued and missing much of his therapy.

"David, Dr. Costabile thinks you'll have to go into the hospital."

"I won't go."

"It'd only be for a few days while they run tests. We have to find out what's causing the fever."

"I'm not going to any hospital."

"You'll have a chance to see everyone I've told you about. Maybe even go into ICU."

"I won't go."

The following morning he completely surprised me. "Tell the doctor I'll go today."

February 13, 1974, at 2 P.M., David and I entered Overlook Hospital.

"Hello, there," called the guard. "How's the boy?"

"David's back," spread like an emergency call. Danny, the inhalation therapist, charged into the room. David didn't remember him, but immediately the two became pals.

I was especially pleased to see the pulmonary specialist drop in. After the introduction, David asked, "What did you do for me?"

"I helped you when you were having trouble breathing."

"In my opinion, David, he helped you more than anyone." The doctor gave me one of those not-really-but-thank-you-anyway smiles.

"I'm glad I stopped in," he said. "He's doing fine."

I knew what he meant. We had talked before David was moved to Kessler. "My main concern," he had said, "is his mind." Now he knew David could talk, think, and understand.

When the hospital chaplain came to visit, David was so impressed that he went to chapel on Sunday. Even after a full year, the organist remembered me and was thrilled to meet David. During the service the chaplain compared individuals to seedlings. He had a display of tiny plants that he had grown from seeds, and gave David a bean plant. Chapel was a happy experience for both of us.

Two nurses who worked in Special Care also came. "David, remember us? I'm Linda and this is Sharon." Studying them carefully and drawing a blank, he finally shook his head "no."

"Every night we'd talk to you."

David was surprised. "Did you really come every night?"

"We sure did. Even when we weren't working in Special Care."

"Sharon," David asked, "will you come to see me at home?"

Linda cut in. "Sharon just got engaged last night."

"Oh well, that's the way it goes." His tone implied, "I tried."

The day before David was discharged from Overlook for the second time, Danny finagled permission from our family doctor to take him into the Intensive Care Unit. It was a Sunday night and the unit was very empty. John and I tagged along. We quietly walked from room to room, showing David his beds, which had been occasionally changed. Danny explained the various machines, equipment, and bottles to David. "Can you remember anything?" he asked.

"Only the beeper box and that everything was white."

One patient seemed to be following us with her eyes. "We're showing David around," Danny said. "He was here in a coma for fifty-three days." Although she didn't respond, I read her expression as, "I hope I'm not here that long." Later, in the hall, I asked David, "What do you think now that you've seen ICU?"

"It's very scary," he whispered, "and I never want to come back."

We had not expected him to be at the hospital a full week, but when one test returned negative they would move on to another, looking for answers. He had every test in the book. The results showed no blockage or stones and the kidney-bladder infection was cleared with a change of antibiotic.

In the meantime, the math tutor did contact David's speech therapist at Kessler and began to give him more challenging work. Both tutors suddenly had a change of heart and agreed David was ready to be given the opportunity to sit in a classroom. We were delighted.

There are five schools in our regional district. One of them accepts fifty handicapped students. An appointment was set up for David and me to visit.

"I won't go," he fussed. "I want to go back to my school."

"They won't take you."

"Why not?"

"Because they have the fire laws and all that jazz to consider."

"They're messed up."

"Maybe so, but that's the way it is. Let's see what the new school is like before we fight the system."

Silently I was disappointed too. I had hoped David could return to his own high school. He had finished his junior year and still knew some classmates. I remembered the second time we had gone to see the principal in vain; we were leaving when a boy walking down the hall called, "Let me get the door for you."

We waited.

"David," he said, "I doubt that you remember me but I was a sophomore when you were a junior. It's good to see you back."

Psychologically, that was the kind of attitude and approach David needed.

The psychologist at David's school rode with us to the special school. It was a half-hour journey from our house. The teachers and staff exuded an aura of warmth. I had the feeling they would be willing to adjust schedules, or do whatever else it might take, to give David a chance. They seemed happy to have him. Their approach was completely the reverse of David's own school. They spoke directly to him and together worked out his schedule. Three afternoons a week he would sit in on a photography and a biology class. David had had both of these classes before his accident, but they wanted to know how much he remembered in order to place him scholastically.

The speech teacher asked, "David, would you agree to meet with me? We'd combine speech and current events. I promise, no drilling."

"Ah, okay."

"Then your schedule's all settled and you will begin on Monday."

"Excuse me," I interrupted, "I have a request. I'd like the math tutor to continue. She's doing so well with David."

Although I had had my doubts in the beginning, she was definitely helping him to advance now.

"The only problem," the director pointed out, "is it would have to be after school hours. We'll ask her if she's willing."

They called her in.

"I'd be glad to continue with David. We're both learning a lot. However, that would mean he'll miss going home on the school bus."

"No problem," I volunteered. "I'm bringing him, so I'll wait."

"For three and a half hours?"

I shrugged. My mind was already racing. With the gas shortage I couldn't go home and come back. Grocery shop? Explore Kenilworth? I'd figure out something.

At the end of the first week I was told that he knew almost as much about photography as the teacher. This was the first year the course was offered in their system. Photography had been David's hobby, and it gave more proof to John and me of his short-term memory returning. The school authorities said he was sociable and happy. It would take a little time for him to settle down, but there were no problems so far.

With spring just around the corner, we decided to cement parallel bars in the back yard for David to practice standing. The only safe place we had indoors was the bathroom, where our plumber had installed a handrail. Clutching John's engineering design of the project, I walked into our local hardware store.

"What can I do for you?" The clerks at the hardware store are always eager to help.

"I need some pipe. Take a look at John's specifications."

"Hmm. What's he trying to make?"

"Walking bars for David. We're going to cement them in the back yard."

"Oh. I don't have everything he needs in stock, but I'll have it by Saturday."

"Fine." Moving toward the exit door, I felt a hand on my shoulder. I turned.

"There'll be no charge on this. We're glad to help out."

At moments like this I was very proud, and felt stronger than ever. The Woman's Club continued to lend support. I had been director of their music department for the past several years. They had asked me to continue, rationalizing that it would be good for me to get out. A list of volunteers who were willing to stay with David during rehearsals was given to me. Others called to say if I needed a few hours out for personal reasons or for one of my previous lecture commitments, they would be glad to come. I was still honoring all contracts my agent had for me as a dramatic book reviewer. When people offered, I accepted.

"David, I'm going to get my hair cut this afternoon. Mrs. Frank is coming."

"Do I know her?"

"Probably not, but you soon will. Maybe she'll play Monopoly with you or help you with your homework."

"I'll ask her." David was always glad for any social contact and accepted whoever came.

John's project was finished. He had done a superior job with the parallel bars. The only problem was that the raw pipe made David's hands and jacket black.

"I'll have to paint them," I moaned.

"Let me do it," David piped up. "I can."

"Okay. What color should we buy?"

"Red."

The first sunny day he crawled along the grass from post to post, painting as he went. It was extremely tiring, just moving his body plus trying to maintain a sitting position while using his left hand, but he finished two posts. The next day he painted the remaining four. As for the barn-red Rustoleum, it was everywhere— on the grass, on the pipe, and on David. Naturally everyone asked, "What's all over your hands?"

"Paint. I painted my walking bars."

Each time he said it, he rose ten feet tall. He wore the color with pride. It was kind of sad to see time and soap wash it away. Each day he practiced standing. In the beginning I clocked him for fifteen minutes before his legs became spastic. Soon his endurance built up to half an hour. David had lots of stick-to-itiveness and continued to increase his standing time.

David had been home five months already. First thing every morning he'd ask, "What day is it?" Today he said, "I think my memory is coming back. Was yesterday Thursday and will tomorrow be Saturday?"

"Yes."

"Then today is Friday and I go to Kessler."

"That's right." Pleased, I leaned over and kissed him. "Now that you have it, hang onto it and don't bug Bonnie for a cane today."

"Why not?"

"Because you're not ready for a cane. You have to force your mind to accept the fact. Otherwise it indicates regression."

"Did I ask for one Wednesday?"

"Yes, you ask every Monday, Wednesday, and Friday. You're like a broken record."

"Okay, remind me not to forget." Unfortunately, David's brain cells seemed unable to receive the message and accept it. I thought of the physical therapists as living saints. And then one day Dr. Sullivan said, "Did I ever tell you that you're a saint?"

"No, but I think you're one too." We were members of a mutual admiration society.

At the special school David had progressed with his math tutor as far as she could take him. He really liked her and cooperated well. On their last day he presented her with a present to show his appreciation.

"I want to thank you too," I said, "for all you have done for David. You brought him a long way."

"I was glad to be able to do it. He did very well and I'm sure he'll continue to move forward." They had finished Math I.

Another math tutor was assigned, and the staff thought David was ready to sit in on a Math I class. I questioned this because he was beyond Math I, but the cold fact came out that it takes a special type of teacher to be able to cope with a handicapped person, and this particular teacher had agreed.

The first day, according to David, he raised his hand and asked, "Would you explain that again? The boy next to me didn't get it." The teacher had just finished explaining the problem with a diagram on the blackboard.

"Who are you to ask me?" she answered. According to David, she made him feel like dirt. He still had some difficulty in being understood verbally, but as luck would have it, his next words came through crystal clear: "You're a stupid jerk."

The class broke up. This only added fuel to the fire, and one minute later David was out of Math I.

"David," I screamed, "you know you don't tell a teacher she's stupid."

"She is, and I'm not going back."

"Don't worry, she won't take you back."

His previous daily routine changed. He was to sit in on a more challenging math class with a man teacher. Actually, the staff felt partly responsible for the disaster and concluded he was still moving onward and upward.

As the months passed the school suggested David come five afternoons rather than three. Their reasoning: His short-term memory was improving slightly, and they wanted to see if he could progress more rapidly with daily repetition. David had been very unhappy with his therapy at the county hospital from the beginning. Now it had advanced to a constant hassle. Weighing the two, I decided to send him to school and give up the therapy.

With our newest schedule it seemed I was forever nagging—eat, brush your teeth, hurry up, we don't have much time.

Within two weeks real problems developed. A girl who had ridden down in the elevator with David ran hysterically crying into the guidance office: "David attacked me on the elevator."

David's version: "Can you believe it?"

"No, but why should she say such a thing?"

"Who knows?"

Then the truth came out. David had put his hand on a girl's knee in class one day. Another day he had put his arm around a girl's shoulder in math class. The photography teacher was afraid to leave him with a girl. They also informed me, "We found him in the parking lot today."

"How did he get there?"

"He left photography class."

"Well, why didn't the teacher stop him?"

No one answered. Instead they inquired, "How often does he see the psychologist at Kessler?"

The psychologist saw no serious problems developing for David. "We know he has self-control," he said. And we both know boys always have and always will be tempted to pinch derrières. David now had to learn that because he was in a wheelchair, society had a tendency to panic. Sad but true.

The chief doctor at Kessler said, "Let us guide you." His tone was comforting. "Go back to three afternoons a week at school. His schedule has become overwhelmingly frustrating. He's seeing himself more and more as he is."

We cut back to the original three afternoons a week, but the damage had been done: David had developed a reputation of having a behavioral problem. The classroom situation did not improve, although he continued to progress with the two tutors. David was tense. I was tense.

"I hate that school. I don't want to go."

"May I remind you, you are the one who wanted to go in the first place."

"Yeah, but I wanted to go back to my school."

The school had asked me to be patient, but I couldn't be patient at David's expense. How I wished I could pick up a book and read ten easy instructions on how to handle this crisis. My worries doubled, tripled. I was discussing it with a friend when she seemed to hit the nail on the head.

"David hasn't missed even one minuscule phase in relearning. Hang in there—so far you've been doing everything else right. You'll figure out what to do."

I wasn't convinced. That night I suddenly remembered what the Big Bear had said to me: "One of these days the man above is going to be looking down and say, 'This girl has had enough.' " I relaxed.

In the morning I knew what to do. I went directly to Kessler's psychologist.

"Things aren't working out at the public school. They really don't have the time, the patience, the teachers, or the facilities to cope with David's multiple problems. We have to find a private school for him to enter by next fall. I want a resident school, too. He can't stand the pressure of going in all these different directions in one day." We'd leave the house at 9

A.M. to get to Kessler, which took one half-hour. From Kessler to the special school it took another half-hour in the opposite direction, and after school another half-hour to get home by 4:30 P.M. It was too long a day.

That decision made, I marched into the specialized school.

"I've decided to bring David only for the two tutors three times a week. And we're looking for a private school for him to enter next fall."

I wasn't sure, but I suspected they were relieved.

A week later I met with Kessler's psychologist again.

"There is only one school for David," he said.

"Oh, really. Where?"

"In Jamestown, North Dakota."

"North Dakota! There must be something closer. Don't we have anything in this big, wide, wonderful metropolitan area?"

Handing me a huge, fat, looseleaf book, he smiled, "Take this home and see what you come up with."

I spent the entire weekend going through private schools with a fine-tooth comb. I was delighted to find two in North Carolina, where our son Lance was attending Bowman-Gray Medical School. There was one in New Mexico, which excited David, one in Pennsylvania near my brother, and one in New York. Beaming, I bounced into Kessler's psychologist's office early Monday morning.

"Okay," he said, "my secretary will sent out letters of inquiry."

Two weeks passed with no word. And then one by one the return letters arrived: "Our school does not meet your son's needs." We had run the full circle and were back to start. My tune immediately changed: "I wish we'd hear from the school in North Dakota."

A week later an application arrived from The Crippled Children's School in North Dakota. David was not happy.

"I want to go far away, but don't send me where they're all in wheelchairs."

"David, we don't have any choice."

The public school located a school in New Hampshire, but in all truth it did not meet David's individual needs as well. The Crippled Children's School is for multiply handicapped students, kindergarten through high school, that the public school cannot handle. The IQ range of the student is 70 and over. The student staff ratio is 96 to 92, thus giving the students more individualized attention. One of the big problems in finding a school was age. David was now nineteen; many schools were for younger children. And for us, the IQ factor was an important consideration. Everyone agreed David needed a challenge, otherwise he became bored and frustrated. When this happened it opened the door to all kinds of complications. Although the school is basically educationally oriented, the students have therapy as a part of their daily routine. For David, we were interested in physical and occupational therapy, which would include prevocational, typing, writing, and so forth, designed to make him more independent, as well as recreational activities in which he could participate. The overall program was ideal for David's needs. Three days later his application was in the mail to the school.

From the time David was discharged to my full care, I never left his side unless he was safely lying in his hospital bed with the sides up. Of course I knew I couldn't protect him every minute, but I didn't want to gamble foolishly. However, I was always searching for a new way to help him improve his coordination, which in itself was a gamble. About this time I was looking for a bicycle exerciser. My friend Lois had one stashed away in her attic and gave it to us.

David was eager to test all my new brainstorms. Immediately he found it wasn't easy to get both legs pedaling together. I kept counting out loud for incentive and rhythm. Twice a day he worked out. Within a couple of weeks he was going great guns, when his feet slipped off the pedals and he tumbled backwards.

What a close call! He had just missed the corner of the piano bench by a hair. We laughed at the funny position he found himself in.

"David, how am I going to get you up?"

"Very simple. You help me."

It wasn't all that simple. Remembering his therapy on the mats he crawled around to a kneeling position and somehow together we got him back into his wheelchair. From then on falls didn't shake us; we merely took them in our stride. He was falling more and more because he was doing more for himself. I recall the day I guided him out the front door with my usual words of wisdom—"Be careful!" One wheel rolled off the sidewalk and David gracefully slid head-on into the evergreens. We were crazily laughing when our worried neighbor came running to assist. But the day he decided to put on his shirt while sitting on the edge of his bed was traumatic. He lost his balance and fell into the stereo, which was on a table next to his bed. I found him lying on the floor with blood spurting all over his face.

"My eye's bleeding," he kept repeating. "Do something."

"David, relax till I get some ice. I can't see what's wrong."

The cut was a thread above his good eyeball and appeared too close for comfort. My heart was thumping as I hurried to the phone and dialed our family doctor. Dr. Costabile was in surgery. I couldn't think.

"Did you get the doctor?" David called. His voice was growing frantic.

And then I knew what to do. "Just a minute, I'm calling our eye doctor."

I was instructed to loosely anchor a bandage over the entire left side of his face and bring him to the office immediately. I was illegally parking in front of the building when the elevator operator recognized David and came running.

"I'll take him right up to the doctor. You park the car."

"Bless you," I answered.

The cut did not affect the eyeball, and a butterfly patch was used rather than sutures. The whole left side of his face was bandaged, diminishing his vision to almost nothing. My heart bled.

"Honestly, David, if it isn't one thing it's another."

"Yeah, well, what can you do?" His tone was flat.

"David," Dr. Romas said cheerfully, "day after to-morrow we'll take the bandage off and you'll be good as new."

Only then did I realize what he had said. The left side of David's face was his normal side, therefore it would heal quickly. God is good.

The 1973–74 public school year ended. David hung on with his tutoring to the bitter end. I had requested a math tutor during summer school and a teacher was assigned. When I called to work out the details she said, "Tell me about David. I understand he's a be-havioral problem."

Oh, hell, I thought, not this attitude again. Why were people so eager to cross him off?

I thundered, "I disagree." Then, knowing I was overreacting, I lowered my voice to almost a pleading cry. "Please treat David as you would any other student. Don't talk down to him. He has a memory problem and is aware of it. If you keep asking, 'Can you remember my name? Can you remember what we did yesterday?' it's extremely frustrating to him. Try to promote recall with association."

She asked for David's present workbook and I agreed to drop it off. By the time we hung up I felt good.

"David, you're going to like your new math tutor."

"What school am I going to?"

"Your school—G.L."

"It's about time."

I was happy too, and sure appreciated the fact that it was only seven minutes from our house.

*   *   *

Our family had been anxiously looking forward to summer, when David could go swimming. Knowing it is the only sport that uses every muscle in the body, we expected great physical progress with water therapy. All our four sons had been competitive swimmers and lifeguards at one time or another. David had been on the high school swim team but had to drop out because of an eye allergy from the chlorine. That fact plus his repeated scratched corneas ruled out any possibility of his going into Kessler's indoor pool. Now, with the coming of June, personal friends offered their heated outdoor pools, which were slightly chlorinated. We gratefully accepted. June 3, a classmate of David's and I took him. Wearing his father's sailing life jacket we helped him bump, step by step, into the shallow water.

"Let go, let go," he snapped. We let go. He flopped around like a fish out of water, coughing and spurting.

"Close your mouth," we called, "you're draining the pool."

Quickly he found out he had to relearn swimming, but he knew what to do and I was thankful for his previous experience. David's sun sign is Taurus. He used to love to read me his astrology prediction in the newspaper, and was proud to have the bull associated with his sign.

"See, I'm strong as a bull." He'd show off by flexing his muscles. Today he seemed to be as he fought to meet his new challenge for over an hour in the water. Exhausted but happy, we went home.

The following day Millie, who owned the pool, suggested a tire inner tube. It was a terrific idea. Inside the tube David's head was above water at all times and he was free to kick his legs and move his arms. Immediately he headed for the deep water.

"David," I barked, "come back!"

"Why?"

"Suppose you slip out of the inner tube? I couldn't bring you up from the bottom of the pool."

"You worry too much."

As Millie and I slipped into the water she whispered, "I know how you feel but his attitude is marvelous."

From then on someone casually was nearby whenever he was in the deep water.

Our summer was incredibly busy. Therapy continued at Kessler on Monday, Wednesday, and Friday mornings. The math tutor and swimming were squeezed in daily. Whether it was cloudy, chilly, or sunny, we went. I shudder when I think what it must have cost Bobbie and Millie to keep their water warm enough for swimming. David would make phone calls to his friends and usually found one to go with us. Of course I needed help getting him into the water, but more important, he needed contact with his peers. What nineteen-year-old boy wants to go swimming with his mother? Each day we saw more and more free movement coming back, especially to his right leg, but no sudden miracles happened. By the middle of July he could bend his right knee up to his chest and kick both legs well. Out of the inner tube, we assisted while he relearned floating and breathing. With a person on each side steadying his balance, he walked back and forth across the pool. David and all of us laughed at his klutziness. However, he could move his legs with less effort in the water and knew with practice his coordination would improve.

The first week of August brought a flood of events. First, summer school ended. The teacher was excellent and together they had accomplished a great deal. Her report was glowing. An excerpt read, "I found David cooperative, polite, and insistent upon correct answers. If he forgot, I only had to give him a hint and he was right back on the track. Some days he did extremely well and others poorly, but he must be challenged. I believe with constant help he can regain all the mathematical skills he had before his accident. We have covered Algebra I and II, factoring, etc."

During the middle of August, David performed a real feat. His lifeguard buddy, Keith, gave the command: "Okay, Dave, today let's see you swim from the shallow part to the ladder in the deep end. Ready . . . on your mark . . . go."

David fell forward with a loud splash, and was unaware of Keith at his side. Although he couldn't reach out his right arm and bring it back through the water, he was able to get his right shoulder above water and bring his head up to breathe. He made it to the ladder. We all yelled, clapped, and showered him with praise. Suddenly Keith yelled, "Dave, what are you doing?"

"Oh, my gosh," I called, "he's swimming back. Stay with him."

We were amazed at his strength. From then on he swam laps back and forth across the pool, increasing the number daily.

One Saturday a letter of acceptance arrived from The Crippled Children's School in North Dakota. David was pleased, we were pleased, and Kessler was pleased. Instantly we had a million and one things to do. Report upon report had to be completed. Appointment after appointment was made. New surgical shoes were ordered. His teeth were examined. We rushed off to our family eye doctor—this time improvement was evident in the left eye. The jump was less and he could read more of the chart. As for the right eye, no change. Sight was very poor; he could only read the big *E* on the wall chart, and the annoying double vision remained, but David was learning to live with it. Unfortunately, neither glasses nor surgery would correct the double vision because it was caused by nerve damage from the original injury. David had been adamant about not using the talking books played on a talking machine that the New Jersey Commission for the Blind had sent through his school system. Now he would have to face the truth. If he couldn't read lengthy assignments, how would he keep up with his classwork? I looked to the new school to help him find alternatives.

His final medical examination showed continued slow progress. The ataxia on his left side had considerably improved; printing done with his left hand was legible. All it took was time. His right side slowly continued to respond. I only stood by while he transferred—he could move both feet into the car, buckle his seat belt, and close the door with his *right* hand. His posture was better, but his dream had not come true: He was still not able to walk, nor did he have a cane. For the past six months or more David had had a cane fixation. Every therapy day at Kessler's he'd demand a cane. I marveled at their patience.

Today, during his examination, he said, "Doctor, I have this hang-up about a cane. Would you write a prescription so I can have one?"

"No, David, you're not ready, but one day you will be. A little more time is needed."

"David," I smiled, "I'm proud of you. If you know it's a hang-up, you've got the problem half licked."

His standing balance had improved, but he could not stand alone. He was relearning at the walking bars, but his gait was still classified as nonfunctional. What gave us encouragement was the fact that he could pick up his own legs and move them. Sitting balance was no longer a problem, nor was speech. He was communicable. We all believed that in the near future no one would detect David had relearned speech.

Shopping was another thing we had to do. Of course, we went to Uncle Vince's store, where we got a discount. I'll never forget David's joy over a new pair of slippers. His first reaction was, "Don't buy 'em. I'll never wear 'em."

"David, they're on the list of things you need to take to school."

Halfheartedly he chose a pair of brown corduroy ones lined with gold terry cloth at a local shoe store. The price was right—$3.99. After we got home he decided to wear them to go swimming. I had to agree, as it really was a pain in the neck getting his socks on over damp feet and then lacing the high-top shoes. He wore the slippers and instantly they became priceless.

After swimming he always rested. Engrossed in my household chores, I passed his bedroom door and stopped dead in my tracks. David was lying on his belly with knees bent and his feet sticking straight up in the air. He had his slippers on. Although he never griped about the rather ugly, heavy, surgical shoes, I now knew what the slippers meant to him, to say nothing of the feeling of joy I had.

To anyone passing by he was a normal boy lying on his tummy. Our family had an aversion to words like "crippled," "handicapped," and "brain damage." David hated the name of his new school, The Crippled Children's. His father intensely disliked the word "handicapped." Darryl didn't like it any better, but in his weaker moments he stumbled over it. Every time I heard "brain damage," I bled a little.

Every day David practiced standing balance and walking at the parallel bars in the back yard. He recognized progress, but it was painfully slow. Naturally he became discouraged. On one of those low days he moaned, "I'm so sick of this whole mess."

"Why don't you call one of your friends," I suggested. "Maybe they'll come over."

He called John and, unknown to me, made arrangements to go over to his house. I didn't know John was recuperating from an operation. When David told me, I asked, "How am I going to get you to John's house?"

"Very simple. You take me."

"Is anyone else at home?"

"No."

"Then how am I going to get you up the steps? John can't lift."

Really annoyed, he barked, "Forget it. I can go by myself."

Before I knew it, he was on his way. He had gone out through the garage and lifted the door himself. I caught up as he was rolling much too fast down the driveway. I reasoned. I pleaded. I yelled. No way would he listen. He kept on wheeling down our sloping street, running into the curb every few feet to brake his speed. The mailman was astounded to see him.

"Dave, where are you going?"

"Over to John's house."

"How are you going to get across Mountain Avenue and up his steep driveway?"

"I'll figure that out when I get there."

Knowing there is a time to speak and a time to keep silent, I kept silent. At the bottom of our street my friend Margie came running out of her house.

Sensing the tense air, she asked, "Dave, are you out walking?"

"I'm going to see John. Do me a favor and keep her here." He pointed to me as though I were a deadly poison.

"I can't do that," Margie said. "She has to go along to see that you get there safely."

Without another word he continued on his way, rounded the corner onto the next street, then stopped. By this time the mailman had caught up with us.

"Better hurry, Dave, looks like rain."

"Yeah," I answered, "it's predicted. Look how dark it's getting. David, be reasonable. You can't possibly make it to John's house and I can't get you up his driveway."

"I can get up myself."

"Okay, then go."

"I'm resting."

"You want a push?"

"Would you?"

"Ask me."

"I'm asking."

"Pick up your feet." We had taken the pedals off

his wheelchair, so he had to wheel himself with his feet and his left hand. In one swift turn I whipped his chair around and headed toward home. He tried to stop me by dragging his feet and letting go with a few choice cuss words, but at the moment I had the strength of a bull. I really don't know how I made it back up the hill. I only know I was breathing heavily and my heart was pounding dangerously fast when we got home. I hurried to the kitchen for water. David called John.

"John, I tried to come over myself, but I couldn't make it." His voice rang with disappointment. I didn't hear what else he said because I wanted to jump up and down, pound my fists, cuss, bawl, anything to release my pent-up emotions. How sad that our nineteen-year-old son couldn't go to his friend's house, a couple of blocks away, by himself. Like a flash an idea struck me.

"David," I called with high-pitched voice, "tell John you'll come over tonight. We'll find someone to take you."

Five minutes later the heavens opened and the rain teemed down. David was exhausted and decided to take a nap. As I was unlacing his shoes my face brightened. I saw humor.

"David, your trip down Holly Glen wasn't all in vain. Look, you wore a hole in your shoe."

"I don't know whether to laugh or cry," he mumbled.

"Laugh. As Father Ashe said, few people are asked to meet your challenge."

After supper Mike took David to John's house.

Almost every night David's friends came over. Sometimes they took him out for a beer, to see a movie, for a ride, or just to someone's house. Other times they played chess at home, listened to records, or talked. These young people were a tremendous boost to his morale. Their faithfulness and their desire to help David warmed our family through and through.

David had just received a note from a group of students at his high school which read, "At the end of the year we find ourselves with a profit from the yearbook. It's too much to keep, so we'd like to give fifty dollars to you."

David was moved. Over and over he repeated, "Isn't that nice of them." He bought luggage for his trip with their money.

Every four to six weeks I received a letter from Oral Roberts. David wrote his own prayer request: "Please continue to pray for me, I'm not walking yet."

People continued to rally around us, too. Friends called to ask, "Would John and you like us to come over tonight? We'll bring the meat and John can cook it on the grill." On special occasions we did go out. Mike or some other friend of David's would come over. A guild organization that had been in touch with me for some time now offered to pay David's plane ticket home for Christmas. After two years people were still doing—not just saying "What can we do," but doing. To know that you are not alone is the greatest comfort of all.

August was speeding by, and with it went the hospital bed. It was disassembled and stored in the garage when we learned David was going away to school. His note to the Woman's Club read, "Thank you for the hospital bed. I used it every night, but now I don't need it any longer." He had slept in it for one year and nine months, and often remarked how comfortable it was. Now his tune changed: "Don't worry, I won't fall out of my own bed."

Once he did. I awoke hearing a thud and a hard bump. Hurriedly I swung out of bed, grabbing my robe. Just then Greg, who was sleeping in David's room, called, "I have everything under control. Dave fell out of bed." Nevertheless I thought I'd better check. I found Greg back in his own bed and David asleep on the floor. Smiling, I nudged David.

"Roll over and crawl back into bed. Come on, I'll give you a hand."

In the morning neither boy remembered a thing.

David had also written to the chaplain at Overlook Hospital. "I want to thank you for the bean plant you gave me. It has become so productive that my mother cooked five beans for me tonight. Enclosed is one so you can see for yourself."

It was 6:30 P.M. David and I were eating when the little blue VW jerked to a sudden stop in our driveway. I couldn't imagine what Darryl and Barb wanted at this hour. Furthermore, we were having a torrential downpour. The door opened and they were inside like a streak. I sensed excitement.

"Where's Dad?"

"He had a dinner meeting tonight. Why?" They both looked like the cat who swallowed the canary.

"We have a family present," Barb said, beaming. "Dave, you may open it." All the while he was getting the ribbon and paper off, instructions were flying right and left—"Be careful, this side has to be up, hurry, we can't wait until you see it." The suspense was killing David and me.

"Let me hold it while you take the lid off," Darryl suggested. And inside, surrounded by fluffy white cotton, was a jagged piece of paper, It read, "We are pregnant."

"I'm gonna be an uncle," David screamed. He was so thrilled and kept repeating it over and over. Suddenly he stopped short, turned to me, and said with great profoundness, "And you, Dot, you're gonna be a grandma."

"In April," Darryl and Barb said in unison.

Sunday, September 1, 1974.

David, John, and I arose at the crack of dawn. Darryl and Barb arrived at 7 A.M. We took family pictures, loaded the luggage into the trunk of the car, and headed toward Newark Airport. David was wound up like a clock, talking all the way.

Our first disappointment came when Darryl and Barb had to stay behind at the security check. They had been with us through it all for over two years. They were the ones who came for Sunday cookouts and helped crank the ice cream freezer. They were the ones who took him to the Bronx Zoo, swimming, or for an airplane ride. Barb had gone with us to shop in Pennsylvania, too. Lance was involved in a summer program through his medical school in North Carolina, and of course came home when he could. Greg had been with us for about five weeks during the summer, but it was Darryl and Barb who were always around —two shining pillars of strength. A big lump popped into my throat when David said goodbye to them. He knew he'd miss them, but his spirits were charged and sparkling as he waved, "See you at Christmas."

At 8:00 A.M. sharp David, John, and I went up the ramp to board American Flight 242. John was allowed to come with us onto the plane.

"David," said the flight attendant, "since we don't have any first class passengers this morning, we're going to let you and your mother ride first class." He wheeled David to the seat directly behind the pilot's section. David said goodbye to his father in a cheerful mood. He was anxious to be off and meet his next challenge.

At 8:30 A.M. the engines trembled. The plane was taking off. David was on his way to The Crippled Children's School in North Dakota to finish his senior year of high school. Actually he only needed two credits to graduate. He would definitely get an accredited diploma and maybe even some extra credits. Who knew? And what was more important, he would be one of the group.

My mind began to drift. It seemed like eons ago I had complained, "I'm bored. All the kids are gone and even David has a job this summer." And then it happened. David's accident. "God," I had asked, "you wouldn't take my seventeen-year-old boy, would you?"

Today, two years and two months later, my daily nursing, chauffeuring, pushing, prodding, guiding, or whatever you want to call it was over. God, in his own time, had brought us to this crossroads. Here we must part—each to his own way.

For me, after my conferences at the school were over, I'd return home to begin anew but with one major change—a different outlook.

For David, probably these next ten months would be his most difficult challenge of all—learning to accept himself as he is and learning to use what he has. But he would do it. Only yesterday our minister had asked, "David, before you leave for school shall we have a word of prayer together?"

"I would like that," he answered.

His outlook had changed too. And I thought about all the young people who had spent so much time with David during these past two years. Their outlook had changed also. David read and reread the plaque Mike had given him last night. "When you reach the end of your rope, tie a knot and hang on."

"That's very good, Mike," he said. "I like it a lot." The two boys exchanged serious looks. "I'm going to take it with me and hang it over my bed. Thanks, Mike."

We were flying high now, right through the fluffy, white, awesome clouds. Even though my eyes were wet, I wasn't upset, sad, or doubtful about David's future. I knew he had a long way to go. God had told me from the beginning—*time*.

The flight attendant interrupted my thoughts.

"David, would you like your breakfast now?"

"I sure would. I'm starved."

The flight attendant smiled and moved his eyes to me. "And what about you?"

"Yes, thank you."

PART FOUR

Home Again

Six weeks later the principal of The Crippled Children's School in North Dakota called.

"Mrs. Landvater, we've decided at our meeting this morning to discharge David. We'd like you to come and pick him up." His tone was final.

"Why?" My heart was racing like mad.

"He's been totally uncooperative, disrupting the classes and giving everyone a hard time."

"Have you told this to David?"

"About two weeks ago we talked in my office, but I haven't told him our last decision."

"When are we to come for him?"

"Anytime this week."

"I'll make the necessary arrangements and call you back." In one phone call, all my high hopes were dashed. My mind was darting like a Ping-Pong ball. I recalled my conference with the director of the school, who was handicapped herself and an inspiration to everyone who met her.

"Receiving a high school diploma will be no problem

for David," she said. "But the adjustment to this type of school will be difficult. Most of our students have had their handicaps since birth and have accepted them. We'll give David until December."

Today was only October 14. And only two weeks ago I had called the principal concerning David's plane ticket for Christmas vacation. He gave me a report.

"He's an expert chess player, I'm told the best we've ever had. Loves to wrestle on the mats, and we have two tutors working with him, but he is having some trouble adjusting."

The report sounded reasonable. Now I wondered, is it possible he deliberately acted up to get kicked out? When he first learned the school accepted him, he teased, "I'm glad I'm going far, far away." However, when we arrived his bright smile evaporated. David had seen many handicapped people since his accident, but had never really considered himself one of them. As the students came in and he spotted their visible handicaps, it was almost too much for him to acknowledge them as peers. Trembling on the verge of tears, he confessed, "This isn't what I'd expected."

"But David, each one is a person first. Their handicaps are secondary. Concentrate on putting out and fully cooperating. Remember what Darryl told you? You can always put out more than you think you can."

He agreed without enthusiasm.

The following morning when we said our goodbyes, David was cheerful. Parents were requested not to see or call their children for six weeks, this being the crucial time of adjustment, but we could write. David's second letter said, "I'm homesick." I took it as a normal turn of events and wasn't especially upset.

Yesterday, relieved that our six-weeks period was up, we telephoned. David sounded great! Darryl and Barb were on the extension phone and not one of us suspected a problem. As a matter of fact, when we hung up we felt sure we had done the smart thing. Now it seemed to be mushrooming into a big mistake. Cold fear wrapped around me like a blanket. I had to find a way out. Weakly clutching my theory that nothing is insurmountable, I dialed Kessler Institute, demanding Dr. Sullivan. After relaying the latest developments, my voice driven by despair, I cried, "Do you have any ideas where we go from here?"

"I was afraid this would happen. He was too far from his family and home. Come in next week and we'll figure out something."

A steadfast calm settled over me and with it came hope, the ultimate wonder drug. Pouring myself a fresh cup of coffee, I finished painting. When the phone rang I had been in the midst of rolling fresh paint on the entrance foyer walls, which were badly scuff marked from David's wheelchair. I have always been a firm believer in work as therapy anyway. Within the hour Ruth, David's speech therapist at Kessler, called.

"I just heard and wanted you to know you're not alone. We're all here to help."

What a comfort! That was the beauty of so many people at Kessler. They had confidence in David and gave him another chance again and again. Fate was with us, too—John was on a business trip and brought David home on his return. I met them at the airport. Beaming from ear to ear, David called, "Hi, Mom!"

I really found it difficult to be cheerful. "What happened, David?"

"Forget that school. It was awful."

"What did you do?"

"Nothing," he laughed.

"I fail to see the humor. What are your plans now?"

"I want to go back to my *own* school and back to Kessler."

His father and I exchanged a sad, helpless look.

Later that night I announced, "David, we're all going to church tomorrow. I'm back in the choir now."

"Okay," was his answer.

Sunday morning I asked our newly appointed minister of youth to come and talk with David. He was young and I was hoping David would relate to him. Steve came Monday night. Immediately David asked,

"Do you want to play a game of chess with me?"

"No, David. I want to talk to you about your life and your future. I want to be your friend, if you'll allow me."

David allowed.

The following week we returned to Kessler. Dr. Sullivan quizzed David about the school. All responses were negative. He had only one thought on his mind—"I want to come back to Kessler and would you write me a prescription for a cane?" A knot in the pit of my stomach swelled and tightened. My worries doubled, tripled, until they spilled out.

"I think we need psychotherapy. What do you think?"

The doctor nodded.

"We'll begin treatment, and when I'm sure David is ready to fully cooperate, we'll return for therapy. Until then no school, no therapy, nothing."

David never said a word. I wasn't sure what he was thinking and I didn't particularly care. It was my responsibility to take the next step.

Two friends recommended Dr. Gent as a private psychiatrist. I called. Quickly he sized the problems as heavy and big. A chill of silence fell over me.

"Well, doctor, if they weren't heavy and big I wouldn't be calling you. The point is, does this case challenge you? Do you want to help David?"

Another chill of silence. Then he flatly said, "Bring David in on Thursday at 2 P.M. That's my day off, but I'll meet you at the hospital."

My voice climbed an octave. "We'll be there!" Hanging up the phone, somehow I knew we had taken a step forward.

Seated across the desk from Dr. Gent, the ugly words kept tumbling on top of each other. I wished he would hush; besides, I had read the report several times. It was terrible. Finished at last, he dropped it onto his cluttered desk.

"According to that, David can't do a thing."

My facial expression registered, Don't you believe it! "David told me he prayed to come home. Do you think he was homesick?"

"I'm sure he was."

"The principal said when he told David they were discharging him, he cried. That's the first time he has ever let his emotions out since the accident."

"Good."

"Doctor, I don't understand the part where they say he was confused?"

"That was due to his totally new environment. It would have passed in time."

"And what about the obscenities he used?" I stumbled over the word.

"At this point David is filled with anger. In brain-damage cases such as his, when they become frustrated beyond their control, they lose their sophistication."

Instantly my mind flashed back to the day our third son called me a bitch. He didn't have any brain damage. "Oh well," I admitted, "David is our fourth son and I'm not the type to get hysterical over a four-letter word, except they aren't a part of his usual vocabulary. I think the biggest problem is how we are going to make him realize he's not ready for a cane."

"It's a fixation. He really needs some medication to help him control his thoughts." Handing me a few sample packets, he continued, "These pills will motivate David to achieve what he wants and make him more reasonable. Let me see him next week."

He stood. Our conference was over. As I tucked the card into my wallet, I noticed he had scheduled David for three appointments. My tension eased. I liked him.

David wasn't sure. "I'm not going to any shrink. I'm not crazy just because I got kicked out of that school."

"David, understand this, you're not going to Kessler, school, or anywhere else until you fully cooperate with Dr. Gent. Got that?"

"When must I go back?"

"One week from today."

No response.

In the meantime, Kessler's psychologist contacted David's regional high school to resume tutoring. We had requested the same math tutor he had during summer school, even though it meant a half-hour drive to her school. It seemed worth the trip because David had progressed well with her. A tutor in English and health was also assigned. Both were at the same school, on a once-a-week basis, starting December 5 from 3:15 until 5 P.M.

Once more David was disappointed and frustrated. The reading-skills workbook presented no challenge. Along the margin he printed, "This book is so stupid."

"David," I reasoned, "don't fight the system. Finish it."

He completed the entire book in one week but spilled his angry feelings out to the psychiatrist. When Dr. Gent questioned me, I pulled the workbook from my handbag, grumbling, "It appears to me that people are compounding David's problems."

The doctor's eyes scanned the workbook. Looking up, he shook his head in agreement. "Have the tutor call me tomorrow. Either she gives him something worthwhile or forget it."

The workbook was changed, but what student can progress with one hour and 45 minutes of tutoring twice a week?

Dr. Gent came to our rescue again. "Let the school get an honor student to help David with his homework. He could even make a new friend. If they won't do that, then ask for another tutor. You know, according to the state laws, he's entitled to five hours a week."

I didn't know. When I relayed the message to the school psychologist, she whined, "We've never done it before and even if we could find an honor student, I wouldn't have a room for them."

"My gosh, there must be some nook in that huge building. If not, give them the furnace room." Her copout annoyed me. In the end, the math tutor was dropped because her schedule couldn't permit more time, and Mr. Jones was assigned. David was delighted because it was a man and from his own high school. I was delighted because his school is only seven minutes from our house. The English and health tutor became hospitalized and was replaced by Mr. Blakely.

Another revised schedule: Monday, Tuesday, and Friday—math tutor in his own school. Wednesday and Thursday—health and English tutor at the school in Clark. The half-hour journey or the waiting for two hours really didn't bug me. I simply did what I had to do. The important thing was that David was receiving his five hours of tutoring per week.

Steve, our minister of youth, had been counseling David every week for an hour or more. Now David decided he would go to the MYF (Methodist Youth Fellowship) group, which met on Sunday evenings at the church. Even though he didn't know these young people, he was eager for the social contact. We drove him to the church; Steve, with some of the boys, returned him. The first night they were all smiles as Steve proudly reported, "David really added to the group discussion tonight."

Overall, things were beginning to look up. It was a welcome respite.

On January 4 a newspaper headline caught my eye. "David, listen to this! The Red Cross is sponsoring swimming classes for the handicapped at the YWCA. One hour every Saturday morning with individual instruction for ten lessons. Want to go?"

"Sure!"

I ran straight to the phone. The voice on the other end was hesitant. "Well, we've never had anyone in a wheelchair before that I know of."

"It's no big deal," I assured her. "I took him swimming every day this summer to private pools. Usually the owner and I bumped him into the water and he backed out the same way. I'll be glad to help, if you like." Two more phone calls and everything was cleared.

The first Saturday, those in charge were amazed with David's performance. He really put out to meet his new challenge, and made no comment about being grouped with handicapped. And the beauty of this program was it only cost ten dollars for ten sessions. My impression of the Red Cross jumped ninety percent. Since parents weren't permitted to watch the swimmers, we spent the hour exchanging our individual problems. Here I was exposed to autistic children, cerebral palsy, muscular dystrophy, and other handicaps. I felt compassion for them and they felt compassion for me. Every week one of the parents rushed forward to offer help in handling David's wheelchair.

Four weeks later Dr. Gent called Dr. Sullivan at Kessler Institute to say that in his opinion, David was ready to return for therapy. Immediately he was scheduled for one hour of physical and one half-hour of speech therapy. David had requested Ruth to help him perfect his speech. He was very happy and assured us he would not bug anyone for a cane. He would channel all his energies into working to achieve a cane. However, on the fifth visit he slipped right back into his old pattern. Unhappily shaking her head from side to side, Ruth wheeled David into the lobby, where I was waiting.

"David was very angry in PT this morning because they wouldn't give him a cane."

Disappointment overwhelmed me. "David, it's the same old story. If you won't cooperate, no one can help you."

"You're so full of shit, it's coming out of your ears." He spit the words out crystal clear. Everyone became a blur as my blood pressure soared. Grabbing his jacket, I shoved it on and raced him outside. As I turned on the car motor, my mouth opened and never closed. Now that I look back on it, I should have had the lecture on tape. Inside the house, still brimming over with anger, I bellowed, "Transfer onto the sofa."

He transferred.

Ripping open the garage door, I spotted two half-filled bags of mix-it-yourself cement. I dragged them inside. Careful to pamper my back, which had been pulled out, I socked them onto David's wheelchair. "I'm sick to death of your talk. That's all you do—talk, talk, talk. I never see any action. Now you're gonna act. Stand up."

With my assistance he stood, grabbing the handles of the weighted wheelchair which was placed in front of him. Releasing the brakes, I barked, "Walk!" Firmly locking my left arm underneath his right arm to help maintain balance, he stepped forward with his left foot. It jerked high in an uncoordinated fashion before it hit the floor. The right foot slowly dragged along. After six steps he stopped, huffing and puffing.

Pleased as punch, he gasped, "Pretty good, huh?"

"Keep moving," I snapped. "You're going to do this three times a day for the next twenty-five days. That will be February 25, the day you have your doctor's reevaluation at Kessler. I'll sit in the wheelchair and you can push me to show them what you can do."

"Good idea," he smiled.

"In the meantime it's a deep, dark secret, and not one word about a cane. Got that?"

He nodded.

That evening David was very proud to show his father his newest achievement. John sat in the wheelchair while David walked from the TV room around the corner to his bedroom and back again.

Dr. Gent had a talent for coming up with new ideas. Today he suggested the Skinner Token Economy System. For David, one day melted into another. If it was a good day, so what? If it was a bad day, so what? With the reward system he would collect tokens and follow his progress or regression on a chart. David considered it a babyish idea, but agreed to give it a try.

The first day he totaled eleven tokens, the second—twenty, the third—twenty-two, the fourth—twenty-seven. However, the fifth day he dropped to fourteen. For the first time he became aware of the days on which he was really working to rehabilitate. Tokens were not easy to come by; however, they were possible in all areas: homework, PT and speech therapy, home exercises, time spent at the walking bars in the back yard, walking by pushing his wheelchair, swimming, performance with the tutors, attending church and Youth Fellowship, plus remembering our grocery list for the speedy check-out counter. The first day he totaled thirty tokens, I asked, "What would you like to have?"

"An eclair!"

Because he had earned it, I was delighted to make his favorite dessert even though he tipped the scales at one hundred sixty-five pounds.

February 2. Communion Sunday.

"David, I have a suggestion. Why don't you go down to the altar this morning and receive communion with your father?"

"I'll think about it."

"It's no big deal unless you make it one. Stay in your wheelchair and then you won't have to transfer to and from the pew."

He wasn't promising anything. Services began. From the choir loft I could see out of the corner of my eye that he had transferred into the pew. That probably meant he wasn't going. The choir received communion first, and then the ushers gave the signal to the members. David transferred into his wheelchair with assistance from his father and came forward to the altar. Hearing a scuffle, I stretched my neck to see him kneeling like all the other parishioners. David selected his own bread cube and grape juice with his left hand from the plate Steve offered. Blinking back a few tears, I saw it as another step of progress. I recalled talking with a mother at Kessler who had a son in a wheelchair from an accident.

"It's five years now," she said, "and Tommy has accepted himself. But it was rough in the beginning."

I knew what she meant.

Exactly two years and seven months after David's accident, he and his cat Herbert slept in his own bedroom upstairs with the new orange and yellow loveflower sheets. David and I agreed, cats aren't so dumb. As long as David remained downstairs in the hospital bed, or later in Darryl's bed, Herbert occasionally would join him. But the minute he was back in his own bed, Herbert was permanent.

"How did you sleep last night, David?"

"Not so hot. I was too excited."

David's room is a far cry from *House Beautiful*. The yellow walls are papered with photos he had taken, developed, and mounted. A mobile of small, round, cut-out pictures hangs from the ceiling. No Parking, and Speed Limit signs add atmosphere. Most important, it has his very own cozy bed.

"Can I sleep here every night?" he begged.

"Only over weekends right now. You still need your father's help to walk up the stairs."

At moments like this I hated our split-level house, except my logical reasoning told me it forced David to try the steps, and that in itself was therapy.

The telephone wouldn't stop ringing. I hurried from the shower dripping wet.

"Mom, this is Darryl. It's a girl, Miranda Ellen, born 6:15 this morning, seven pounds three ounces, nineteen and a half inches long. She's not red and ugly at all, and has lots of hair."

He finally took a breath. "A girl! That's terrific! How's Barb?"

"Fine. Everything went as scheduled. I saw it all."

So the LaMaze method really works?"

"Oh yeah. When are you coming up?"

"I hope soon."

Darryl and Barb had moved to Williston, Vermont, only a month ago. Unfortunately Vermont is not just a skip and a hop away, but somehow we'd figure out a way to see our new granddaughter. "David," I shouted, "you're an uncle!"

And then another miracle happened. We were playing bridge with our friends Isabelle and Jim when David called, "Mom, come here!" His tone was urgent.

Running to his downstairs bedroom and trying to sound calm, I asked, "What's up?"

"My right foot's cold."

"Is that all? I'll get another blanket."

"No, you don't understand. I can feel my right foot's cold."

"David, that's tremendous! It means that sensation is returning to your foot. Let's cover it up and keep it toasty warm."

A few days later David was sitting at the kitchen table waiting to be served dinner when he realized, "You know, I can see that picture with my right eye." It was a still life facing him on the wall above the table.

"Cover your left eye and tell me what you see."

"A coffee grinder, a mug, and I don't know what the other thing is; it's white."

"It's a napkin. Gee, that's amazing, David. Are you still seeing double?"

"Yeah."

"Hang in there and dream big." We had been hoping the double vision would soon end. It could take up to five years or it could remain throughout his life. Lance had told us of a student he knew in college who had double vision; still she had learned to read and kept up with her class. The story had impressed us. If she could do it, why not David, if he had to.

The very next evening, during dessert, David suddenly coughed. "Boy, this coffee's hot. I feel it right here." He pointed to his right cheek.

"It seems to me the sensations are returning on your

whole right side, David. Let's see what the doctor says next week during your reevaluation."

Nothing was easy or fast for David to accomplish. Time and again I found myself crying, "Help us, God. Give us the patience and the strength to go on day by day." I had programmed myself not to worry about the future. Since January David had been faithfully walking every day in back of his wheelchair, using our neighbors' driveway because it was more level. Two neighbors—Ingrid and Monique—alternately volunteered to sit in the chair to weight it. Locking my left arm underneath David's right arm to assure balance, we walked. Once he mastered the trip down we turned around and walked up. Now, four months later, David was ready to show Kessler what he had achieved.

Big John, one of the orderlies, sat in the wheelchair as three doctors observed David's surprise. However, I hadn't counted on the fact that John weighed twice as much as either neighbor or that David would be terribly excited. These unexpected factors caused his wobbly balance to be extra shaky, and he really didn't walk half as well as he did at home. However, the doctors agreed that the sensations were returning to his whole right side and he should continue walking. All were pleased.

Still feeling high, David asked, "Now do I get a walker?" He had sort of given up on the cane idea.

"No, David, but one day your dreams will be realized."

Nevertheless, the bomb had dropped. No matter how much overall praise the doctors gave him, he was blue. Not me! David had proven what he could do on his own. I considered it a big step forward, and no question about it, others would follow. As my father had said many times, "I never see David going backwards."

Time passed. It was the end of the school year. David had progressed well with both tutors. Suddenly, after two years, the school arranged a meeting with Dr. Kenny, director of specialized education for our regional system, David's school psychologist, Carol Regal, and myself. We met at David's school.

The doctor spoke first. "Mrs. Landvater, we want you to know that whatever David's educational needs may be, we are here to help." His voice was most sincere. "But I'm not sure," he continued, "that I know what it is you're looking for."

Our eyes locked. He had just burst my beautiful bubble.

"I'm looking for the same things for my son that you're looking for for your son—an education to prepare him for his future."

"David can have his diploma now, you know."

"I don't want it. If you're saying David isn't doing well, he can't go any further, then I'd accept it. To date every tutor has noted progress. Last week Kessler retested him and his verbal IQ is now over ninety. I do want to give full credit to Ben Jones, David's math tutor, who is truly an outstanding teacher—the best David has had. From the very beginning he expected performance and he received it. I didn't find that kind of a positive attitude from the specialized teachers."

"May we have your permission," the psychologist cut in, "to write to Kessler for the test results?"

"Of course."

"Will you accept the diploma in January?" Now I felt he was boxing me in.

"No way. You and I both know this is the last year the public system is responsible to educate David. He turns twenty-one in May, but right now he needs and deserves the benefit of the full year."

In the end I was disappointed with our conference. The doctor was very pessimistic about the possibility of locating a special school for David to attend in the fall, although he did agree to schedule a math tutor during summer school.

With summer around the corner, I contacted the Clover Hill Swim Club, where our family had been past members, requesting a single membership for David with the stipulation that we would hire a lifeguard to instruct him. Clover Hill is a man-made lake with lots of space, so scheduling could be flexible. Once again we were shot down. The club had its insurance and other problems to think about. Experience, on the other hand, had taught me that if one avenue comes to a dead end, try another.

"David, let's get a seasonal ticket at the Berkeley Heights Community Pool for you."

"Good idea," he answered.

Immediately I called the pool manager. "Of course we'll sell David a membership. No problem."

I found myself questioning, "Are you sure the board will agree? What about insurance?"

He merely answered, "Go into the office and fill out an application. It's open every morning."

David was thrilled. "Let's go down right now, and I'm walking in."

He had a walker. When the walking became easier by pushing the weighted wheelchair, we eliminated the neighbors and went back to the two cement bags. The day David said, "I don't want any weights in the wheelchair; I'm gonna walk into my own driveway," was the day the walker became a reality.

"Well, please understand you'll have to walk up the road to our driveway, and you can't change your mind in midstream."

"I can do it." He was feeling like Taurus the bull.

"If you can, I'll get you a walker."

"Okay, let's go."

Going up the hill was hard work. The wheelchair repeatedly tipped backward from David's uncoordinated balance. I had visions of both of us rolling to the bottom in a mangled heap. Our road is a cul-de-sac, which cuts traffic, but a car came speeding along, adding more tension. We were so busy that we couldn't look up. I had a funny feeling the driver's eyes were fixed on us, wondering what we were trying to do. It was David's sheer determination that made it possible for him to get to my parked car in our driveway. I opened the door. With legs shaking from total exhaustion he grabbed the car door and flopped into his wheelchair.

A promise is a promise. The very next day we went to the surgical supply store and bought a walker. Of course he couldn't use it independently, but it was a beginning and a super ego booster. One simply had to try new things. That's rehabilitation.

The next day we took the walker to the community pool. David walked through the gate to the office. Utterly spent, he dropped into a nearby chair. At that precise moment a lifeguard stepped out of the locker room and stopped.

"Aren't you Dave Landvater?"

"Yeah. Aren't you Will Benson?" David asked.

"Yeah. I remember you from school. I work here as a guard."

"Oh, great," I interrupted. "I'm looking for a guard to instruct David. We're getting him a membership today."

"I'd be glad to work with Dave."

"Good—I'm willing to pay the going rate."

We took our application and went home. Another thing I had learned through experience: People are strange. Either they went out of their way to become involved with David or they turned their heads, pretending not to see. Will saw.

The following day, as David and I were struggling with the walker (he wanted to use it wherever we went and I let him when we had time) into the school building, a student rushed up.

"Are you Mrs. Landvater?"

"Yes."

"I'm Will Benson's brother. He wants me to be sure and tell you that he'll work with Dave at the pool any day, for free."

David and I were speechless.

That night the thought occurred to me that it might be wise for Will to see how the instructors at the YWCA handled David. Will's brother covered for him during working hours so he could come. Bill, another fine person who became personally involved with David, took Will into the water and showed his routine. I watched from the bleachers. The YWCA, like Kessler, sometimes had elastic rules. Originally we met Bill as a volunteer water instructor at the handicapped classes. When I wanted to increase David's water therapy to twice a week, Bill agreed to work with him every Tuesday night. Sidney was another who faithfully worked with David on Saturday mornings. Being a peer, he communicated well with David.

David's friend the Big Bear recommended the A. Harry Moore Laboratory School in Jersey City as a possibility for David to attend in the fall. Mr. Flaherty, a professor, had come to see David at Overlook Hospital and had been keeping track of him ever since. He drove us to the school. David seemed pleased with the teachers and the administrative personnel that he met. In fact he discussed some tentative subjects and said he would like to come back in the fall. It was the consensus that we needed to locate a school nearby where David could attend as a part-time student while continuing his physical therapy. I was sure hoping I wouldn't have to drive into Jersey City every day. It's a two-lane road with bumper-to-bumper traffic in the peak hours, but of course deep down inside I knew I would do what I had to do.

Kessler decided David needed a break from therapy. It wasn't that he was uncooperative, but rather that he had come as far as they could bring him at the present time. He had plateaued. On June 1, 1975, after three years, the Kessler Institute of Rehabilitation closed the David Landvater file. We simply said goodbye to the outpatient doctor and left. It did not come as a shock. For a month we had known that he was going to be discharged. However, it was David's dream to leave Kessler walking. True, we had a walker at home, but we had never brought it to Kessler. One had to be realistic. Using the devices took lots of time and patience. Since this was his last day, I gave in to his dream and brought the walker with us. It was waiting in the outer lobby. Kessler's new extension wing had been completed, giving the outpatients a private section. I wheeled David to the lobby, where he stood and with my assistance walked toward the automatic doors.

"David," Claire called, "you're walking!" She was bubbling over with joy.

"Yeah." His tone was weak and negative.

"David's being discharged today, Claire, and it's tough to break the ties. He's been here so long he's become a fixture."

"David," Claire suggested, "why don't you go to the new Kim Institute?"

"I'm not sure we can afford it," I volunteered. "We're running out of money." Nevertheless, she planted the thought. Claire is a beautiful young mother who has been persistent for the past six years in regaining her ability to walk. Her attitude is fabulous. For a short period she was an inpatient, but now, like David, is an outpatient. She had just arrived for her therapy. Claire and other friends cheered as David walked to my car.

After lunch David was exercising on the living room floor, listening to records, when he called me.

"I've decided to go to the Kim Institute. I really want to. Will you take me?"

"Well, David, we've never had another opinion." In my own mind I had wondered what would I do when Kessler finally said, "This is all we can do." Now they had said it. I had collected a storehouse of possibilities —why not try one of them?

"Okay, David. I'll call for an appointment to have you evaluated."

July 5, 1975, 2 P.M. David and I entered the Kim Institute of Rehabilitation Medicine. It had opened only five months ago. Dr. Kim, the medical director, examined David. He was very efficient and thorough as he dictated to his secretary David's limitations and problems from head to foot. I sat there silently hoping and praying this doctor would feel he could help David further, but I also had to be ready to accept the fact that maybe he couldn't. Weighing the two thoughts, I came to the conclusion that for the past three years I'd been surrounding myself with positive thoughts, so why change now?

Finished. Dr. Kim looked directly into David's eyes. "You've come a long way, but I believe you can go further. Not without hard work, though, and I mean hard work. Are you willing?"

"Sure." David's answer was quick and strong.

Now it was my turn to come into conference. Together we agreed David would begin physical therapy every weekday morning, and three times a week he would have an acupuncture treatment. I was eager for David to try these treatments. David had mixed emotions, but consented.

Our previous schedule was revised. Monday through Friday we left the house at 7:45 A.M. and drove to the Kim Institute in East Orange for physical therapy from 8:30 to 9:30 A.M. The days we had acupuncture, our stay was longer. After lunch David had summer school from 1 to 3 P.M. Unfortunately, Mr. Jones was not available to tutor David; however, he personally found a replacement. We met Mr. Wayne at David's high school. The school atmosphere pleased David, and the library was comfortably air-conditioned. After his tutoring, he went swimming at the community pool. It was a strenuous schedule for both of us, lots of ins and outs of the car as we were continually on the go, but David was happy.

The atmosphere was highly charged the day David got his first acupuncture treatment. Dr. Chow inserted five needles—top of head, each leg near the knee, and each arm near the elbow—then set a timer for fifteen minutes. David did not feel the needles; in fact they seemed to have a calming effect. He simply closed his eyes and let the time drift by quietly. However, once home he became very active—I want to do this and I want to do that—and I let him.

After three acupuncture treatments David's right hand, which he held fisted most of the time, became less rigid. We had hoped the treatments would ease his ataxia and relax him so the physical therapist could do more. Dr. Chow saw David daily in PT. Following the fifth treatment he admitted, "David seems to be responding." In the beginning Dr. Chow had been doubtful that the acupuncture would help because the initial accident had been slightly over three years ago. But I was counting on the fact that his right side had only recently begun to return.

Time has a habit of dragging when one has nothing in particular to do. While David had his therapy I waited in the lobby, chatting with a woman who was also waiting. She told me about her husband's mouth cancer and how the acupuncture gave him relief from pain for the first time in over a year. Now he could enjoy eating again. I shared her joy.

And then I asked the security guard for directions to the personnel department. Oozing all the charm I could muster, I announced, "I come to the institute every morning for an hour and I'd like to volunteer my time."

For a minute Mr. Hess stood perfectly still as though in a trance, then smiled. "That's marvelous! Let me introduce you to Barbara. She'll place you . . . Thanks for coming in."

Barbara gave me the key to operate the patient elevator. To tell you the truth, I hadn't planned on becoming an elevator operator. But one thing was certain, I had finally reached the saturation point with human tragedies. I needed a break. David told everyone, "Listen to this. My Mom's an elevator operator. Isn't that funny?"

A week later a call came from Personnel. I had butterflies in the pit of my stomach—I'm from the generation that believes when the boss calls, you're in trouble.

"Dorothy," Barbara said, "we need a volunteer downstairs to open the cafeteria. We serve coffee and danish to our staff, visitors, and guests from 9 to 11 A.M. Would you be willing to do that?"

"Certainly." I was never quite sure if it was a promotion or a demotion. But I do know for a fact that I was the only volunteer who arrived every morning at 8:30 A.M. sharp. I loved my new job, and to this day I'm still serving coffee.

David had been swimming at the community pool every day the weather permitted, and take my word for it, the summer of 1975 was hot and humid. After the second week Mr. Carpenter, the manager, approached me.

"Mrs. Landvater, on Will's day off, bring David anyway. We have other guards who would like to work with him."

"Gee, that's terrific!"

"And you don't have to take him home right away. Let him stay for a while. Be good for him."

It seemed to be part of the plan that different people continually stepped forward to help David. From then on he stayed at the community pool between one and two hours. One overcast, cool day I found him sitting behind a makeshift table-desk inside the pool entrance.

"Guess what, Mom?" His voice was highly charged.

"What?"

"I have a volunteer job, too!"

"Oh, really? What are you doing?"

"As the people come in I ask, 'May I help you?' And then I take their money, give change and a badge."

"Very good, David."

"And Mr. Carpenter's giving me a job next summer." His eyes were sparkling.

"Doing what?"

"Working here at the desk. He's gonna pay me, too."

"Huh, I don't get paid for my volunteer job. You're pretty lucky."

"I sure am."

*   *   *

Another reevaluation. Another wait. Six weeks had
sped by since David had begun his daily therapy at the
Kim Institute.

"David," Dr. Kim said, "you're showing definite
signs of improvement in all areas." Turning to me, the
doctor continued, "I recommend another fifteen acupuncture treatments. We'll keep the physical therapy
as scheduled, but now I want to add hydrotherapy.
David will go into a big heated water tank with bars
where he can practice walking."

For a fraction of a second I cringed at the thought
of coming every morning for another five weeks. The
trip took forty-five minutes one way, and David's starting time was 8:30 A.M. sharp. Then the impact hit—
what was wrong with me? I came here hoping and
praying for progress and now six weeks later we had it.

"Fine," I nodded in complete agreement. And that
night I bought five hundred brewer's yeast tablets. Why?
Exhaustion.

Another phone call from the school psychologist.

In order to bring their records up to date, the study
team needed to retest David. The learning-disabilities
teacher asked that we schedule three separate sessions
because David tired quickly. I was tempted to disagree,
but since I didn't fully understand the extent of the
exams, I sandwiched three appointments into our week-
ly routine. David wasn't one bit up-tight about the
retesting. In fact, he seemed eager to go, and on D-day
was definitely psyched to prove his abilities. An hour
later the learning-disabilities teacher came running out
to my car smiling.

"We're finished! It's remarkable how much he's
improved."

"You mean I don't have to bring him back again?"

"No. We completed everything this morning." Her
voice expressed surprise.

"You'll let me know the results, won't you?"

"Oh, yes."

*   *   *

A few days later Mr. Jones, David's math tutor, proudly straightened his shoulders and said, "Maybe I shouldn't be telling you, but I can't keep it in. David's IQ tested 103."

Words cannot describe his joy, David's joy, or my joy. David was normal. Another miracle. Another day of rejoicing. Months later I was informed the study team withdrew "neurologically handicapped" and reclassified David as "orthopedically handicapped."

Newspaper headline: "Dessert Card Party Benefit for Local Youth. The Woman's Club of Berkeley Heights is continuing preparations for the dessert card party for the David Landvater Fund, to be held June 13, 1975."

This being the second card party they sponsored, David wanted to go. Together we entered with his walker. Everyone was very impressed to see David on his feet. He had rehearsed his speech often, and when the time came to give it, he stood—and slipped. The ladies panicked, with an audible, "We can see him just fine."

But David and I never accepted false starts. "It's okay," I assured them. "The floor is slick; bear with us as we try again." Success.

"Well, ladies," David said, "thank you very much for coming." Pleased, he sat down and enjoyed his dessert. It was only one sentence, but it was executed with perfect diction. The benefit netted eight hundred dollars. David and I both felt extremely fortunate that after three years, people in our town still were giving their time, their gifts, and their money. At moments like these I felt if I lived to be a hundred, I would never forget these acts of love.

The summer of 1975 was the happiest and most satisfying for David since before his accident in 1972. He seemed to thrive on his super-busy schedule, and rain or shine we went to the community pool daily. Even on wet, chilly days the staff included David. They played chess or cards or all went over to someone's house. What a wonderful group of young people! The adults, too, showered David with empathy. Many times during the adult swim time the guards took David into the water. On those hot, humid, overcrowded days everyone willingly moved aside to give David the space he needed. One day I asked the manager, "Does anyone fuss about the fact that David goes into the water for his instruction during the adult swim?"

"No," he answered firmly, "and they'd better not, or out they go."

On closing day, to show his deep appreciation, David proudly passed around a batch of homemade fudge that he had made. It was delicious. And to show my deep appreciation, I gave each staff member a silver dollar as a good-luck charm. It was Will who asked, "Mrs. Landvater, have you heard what we're doing with our silver dollars?"

"No."

"We're hanging them in our cars."

My prayer was silent: Please God, protect each one.

With the passing of summer, the school psychologist made an appointment to enroll David at the A. Harry Moore School in Jersey City. The day was stifling, the traffic horrendous. Arriving late, we hurried inside only to wait in cramped hot quarters of the secretary's office on the second floor, directly opposite the elevator. Within minutes the staff started to organize the younger students for dismissal. Although some were walking with aids, many were in wheelchairs. David gave his undivided attention to the whole procedure. His eyes were glued on the handicapped students as they were moved forward and loaded onto the elevator. When the doors slammed shut for the last time and the halls were quiet, David made his decision. Turning to me, he said, "I'm not gonna like it here." His tone implied that nothing could change his mind.

The principal's door opened and we were called inside.

"David," he asked, "what courses would you like to take?"

"Math."

"Fine. We'll schedule you for Algebra I."

The school psychologist jumped in. "David's being tutored in Algebra II now."

"Oh, then he's had more math than we can offer."

"What courses can you offer David?" I asked.

"How about French? We find for those who have speech problems, a language is very helpful."

"I don't want French. I've already had two years of German." David was growing annoyed.

"I think you'd be pleased with our wood-workshop course, David. We have an excellent teacher."

"I've had enough of workshops."

My eyes drilled holes into David's, silently screaming, "You'd better change your attitude." Turning to the principal I said, "It was my understanding that you had received David's records and would have a tentative schedule for us to discuss."

"On the contrary. I'm working in the dark."

In the end he said he would accept David for half days although it was highly irregular, and the only unsettled detail remaining was which subjects David wanted to take. We said we'd be in touch, and left.

The following day, as David and I returned from therapy, the phone was ringing, ringing, ringing. It was the school psychologist.

"Mrs. Landvater, are you still planning to send David to the school in Jersey City?"

"No. I'm sure you could tell from David's attitude yesterday that it won't work. We'll have to go back to tutoring. Mr. Jones has told me he'd be happy to tutor David in math again. Please set it up. Also, I've been wondering, don't you have some kind of a class that David could be a part of? Music, for example."

"As a matter of fact, we do have a music appreciation class. It's new this year, with only four students. I'll ask the teacher if he would be willing to take David."

"Good. And David would like to have biology and

physics, too. See what you can do so we have our allotted tutoring time per week."

David's most faithful disciple, Mr. Jones, spoke up for him at their staff meeting.

"Give David a chance, that's all I ask. He studied math with me last year and continually improved. It was ridiculous that his mother had to take him to the school in Clark when we have excellent teachers here. He deserves to come back to his own high school."

Mr. Dietrich gave David that chance by accepting him into his music appreciation class. And it was Mr. Jones who found a biology and physics tutor, Mr. Fox. Mr. Fox had taught all four of our sons, and was eager to have David as his pupil. Both tutors requested their textbooks in large print, which was made possible through the cooperation of the New Jersey Commission for the Blind.

Another revised schedule. Beginning September 10, Monday through Friday at 2 P.M. David attended the music appreciation class in his own high school. At 3 P.M. Larry, a classmate, pushed David down the hall to Mr. Jones's classroom for tutoring. David was so thrilled to be there that he didn't argue about taking the walker, but agreed the wheelchair was more practical. I picked him up at 4:30 P.M. It was a full day, with his therapy in the morning, but he had won his heart's desire—he was back in his own high school.

During the second week Mr. Bartlett, the band instructor, stopped me in the hall. Smiling and shaking his head, he admitted, "I can't believe it. It's amazing how far he's come! I still remember what he looked like at Overlook Hospital. I was sick for days. I've been wondering, what can David do with his right hand now?"

"It's coming around. He's just starting to use it to aid his left hand."

"If you think I could help, I'd like to see David pick up his drumsticks again."

"So would I. I'll ask him today."

Driving home, I said excitedly, "David, Mr. Bartlett is so pleased with your progress that he would like to give you private drum instructions. What do you think?"

"Really? He would do that for me?"

"Sure. Remember, you were first drummer for him at one time."

"I'll go in tomorrow." His voice rang with enthusiasm.

The next day when I picked up David at the school, he was glowing. "Look what Mr. Bartlett gave me."

"New drumsticks and a practice pad."

"Yeah. And there's no charge."

"Terrific! He's a man after my own heart."

"So tomorrow bring me fifteen minutes earlier. I'm gonna go every day. Okay?"

"Okay."

I realized the time had come for me to step back and let others step in. I felt eternally grateful to those who did, accepting it as part of the plan for David.

Words of praise and thanks must be given to Herta, David's physical therapist at the Kim Institute. David was a challenge to any therapist, and Herta took that challenge to heart. A couple of weeks after David began therapy with Herta, she told me, "Yesterday I went over to Kessler Institute and talked with the PT Department. I wanted to learn more about David and how I might further help him."

I was impressed that she would take the time and effort to do that. Herta is a busy young mother with two small children of her own. A short time later she explained some new ideas in therapy she had discovered by researching articles about cases similar to David's. Herta also understood that the exact same routine day in and day out caused boredom to settle over David like a fog, and with it came an unwillingness to cooperate.

"I'm so sick of exercising on these mats," he'd grumble. "I'm not gonna do it."

Herta continually let him try new things, but was

firm when repetition was necessary. Several times a week she'd come through "my" coffee line in the cafeteria, giving a report and always encouraging me to come into PT to observe so David would have carryover at home. Over and over I'd remind David, "You're very fortunate. You've had some of the finest professional people working with you. Appreciate it and give your all because you only receive when you give." My lectures were constant. The minute I saw him slipping mentally or physically I'd jump in with advice to pick him up and move him forward. Of course it didn't always work, but I never missed the opportunity.

Reggie, an assistant in PT, also deserves tremendous credit. Daily he helped Herta with David, and twice a week took him into the big water tank to practice his walking. As he gave the commands, David followed through as though he were hypnotized. From the first time the two boys met they communicated, and their relationship grew into a deep friendship.

The day—October 16, 1975. The time—2:30 P.M. The event—another reevaluation.

Dr. Kim was happy to see progress. David could now balance himself on hands and knees without falling over. He could shift himself rhythmically in the kneeling position. His sitting balance had improved and range of neck motion was complete. He could now extend his right arm between 90 and 150 degrees, depending on the amount of spascitity. However, David was learning to control involuntary movements. His right hand was beginning to function as a useful part of his body; it had developed strength and he could open and close his fingers. The overall ataxia was more controlled and his short-term memory was getting better too. David's weight dropped to 162, a loss of six pounds, but best of all, he had begun to stand alone. Just for a minute at a time, but it was a beginning.

Red letter day—November 8. David swam the length of the YWCA pool for the first time. It was quite a feat to behold and I missed it. One of the mothers told me unashamedly how the tears ran down her face as she watched. When I made an appearance, David yelled, "I swam the length of the pool. But you tell her, Sid, so she believes me."

On the way home he said, "It really felt good swimming this morning . . . To think I didn't want to come."

"I'm glad you admitted it, David, because today you made two steps of progress."

At school, the music teacher was ready to quiz the class. He didn't know what to do about David, but David solved the problem.

"I want to take the quiz too."

The test was given verbally and David answered verbally. I quote the teacher: "I graded David and he earned an A. He was extremely pleased, as was I."

A's became contagious. In his math quizzes for three consecutive weeks he scored a 90, 83.4, and 100. Mr. Fox, the biology and science tutor, classified David as a B-to-A student. Another wonderful thing happened —some of the students started to include David. Larry and his friends took him to a chorale concert, and several weeks later to a play, both at the high school. David was beginning to relate to his peers. I noticed when I took him into the band room that he knew students by name, and on occasions when Mr. Bartlett wasn't available to instruct him with the drums, one of the boys would offer. "Leave Dave with us. We'll take him to his music class."

And then just before Christmas Mr. Jones asked me to come into his classroom for a minute before he began tutoring David. He looked like the cat who swallowed the canary. I wondered what was up.

Beaming like a Cheshire cat, he said, "At our staff meeting yesterday we decided David is legitimately earning credits this year towards his high-school diploma."

Turning to David, he continued, "You're going to graduate this year with the class, David, and receive a regular diploma."

"I will!" David shouted.

I heard Mr. Jones answering David, but they lost me. The beautiful scene I had expected one day was before me now—David in his royal blue cap and gown would be sitting in a chair on the platform, probably in the front row. When they came to the L's, I'd snap to attention, straining to hear *David Ashley Landvater.* David would stand up, extend his left hand to receive his diploma, and shake with his right hand. Maybe it would take a minute or two longer, but that would only heighten the excitement of this momentous occasion. John would snap the camera and I would sniffle. This wasn't just another son's graduation from Governor Livingston Regional High School. This was our fourth son. Our son—who the experts said would not live. Our son—who does not hear. Our son—who does not see. Our son—who will be retarded. Our son—who if he does speak will have a limited vocabulary. Our son —who will never be the same. In that respect, they were right. For David had lived through this horror; he had faced fear. He did what he had to do even though he thought he couldn't do it. The night of the accident I had asked God, "You wouldn't take my seventeen-year-old son, would you?"

Time was my answer. And time was still with David. Time had not run out. Time stretched before David like the ocean. He couldn't see the other end, but he knew it was there—*time.*

"Mom," David shouted, "didn't you hear what Mr. Jones said? I'm gonna graduate this year." Startled back to reality, I kissed the top of David's head. "I heard. I was thinking about what Father Ashe told you. Remember? He said, 'This accident has created the biggest challenge in your life that you will ever have to face, but I know you can do it.' "

"You did it, David. You did it."